My Name Is Immigrant

Other Books by Wang Ping

Life of Miracles along the Yangtze and Mississippi, creative nonfiction, University of Georgia Press, 2018 (2017 Association of Writers and Writing Programs Award for Creative Nonfiction)

Ten Thousand Waves, poetry, Wings Press, 2014

The Dragon Emperor: A Chinese Folktale, children's folklore, Millbrook Press, 2008

The Last Communist Virgin, short stories, Coffee House Press, 2007 (2008 Minnesota Book Award for Novel & Short Story, 2007 Association for Asian American Studies Book Award for Poetry/Prose)

The Magic Whip, poetry, Coffee House Press, 2003

Aching for Beauty: Footbinding in China, cultural study, Random House, 2002 (paperback); University of Minnesota Press, 2000 (University of Colorado's Eugene M. Kayden Award for Best Book in the Humanities)

Of Flesh & Spirit, poetry, Coffee House Press, 1998

Foreign Devil, novel, Coffee House Press, 1996
Translated into German as *Fremder Teufel*, Peperkorn, 1997

American Visa, short stories, Coffee House Press, 1994 (1996 New York Public Library Book Award for the Teen Age)
Translated into Dutch as *Vossengeur*, Uitgeverij de Prom, 1997
Translated into Japanese as アメリカンビザ, Kadokawa Shoten Publishing, 1994

Books Translated by Wang Ping

Flash Cards: Poems by Yu Jian, poetry, co-translated with Ron Padgett, Zephyr Press, 2010

New Generation: Poems from China Today, poetry anthology, co-translated with Ron Padgett, Anne Waldman, Lewis Warsh, Dick Lourie, and others; Hanging Loose Press, 1999

Flames: Poems by Xue Di, poetry, co-translated with Keith Waldrop, Paradigm Press, 1995

My Name Is Immigrant
我叫移民

Wang Ping
王屏

Hanging Loose Press
Brooklyn, New York

Cover design: Wang Ping
Cover photograph: Tom Wallace
Additional photographs: Wang Ping
Title/author typeface (Ava Divina) and wave graphic design:
K. Sobanja at Ava Creative
Design, production and marketing associate: Jesse Katzman

Hanging Loose Press thanks the Literature Program of the New York State Council on the Arts for a grant in support of the publication of this book.

Published by Hanging Loose Press
231 Wyckoff Street
Brooklyn, New York 11217-2208
www.hangingloosepress.com

Printed in the United States of America
10 9 8 7 6 5 4 3 2 1

ISBN 978-1-934909-66-9

Table of Contents

—this book is dedicated to immigrants everywhere—

things we carry on the sea

we carry tears in our eyes: good-bye father, good-bye mother
we carry soil in small bags: may home never fade from our hearts
we carry names, stories, memories of our village, our civilization
we carry scars from proxy wars of greed
we carry carnage of mining, droughts, floods, genocides
we carry dust of our families incinerated in mushroom clouds
we carry our islands sinking under the sea
we carry our hands, feet, bones, hearts and best minds to start
a new life

we carry diplomas: medicine, engineer, nurse, education, math,
poetry, even if they mean nothing to the other shore
we carry railroads, plantations, laundromats, bodegas, taco trucks,
farms, factories, nursing homes, hospitals, schools, temples . . .
built on our ancestors' backs

we carry old homes along the spine, new dreams in our chests
we carry yesterday, today and tomorrow
we're orphans of the wars forced upon us
we're refugees of the sea drowning in plastic wastes
we came from the same mother in Africa
we're your children, sisters and brothers, father and mother

our tongues carry the same weight as we chant

爱 (ai), حب (hubb), ליבע (libe), amour, love
平安 (ping'an), سالم (salaam), shalom, paz, peace
希望 (xi'wang), أمل ('amal), hoffnung, esperanza, hope, hope, hope

as we drift . . . from dream to dream . . . sea to sea . . .

I. Old Home | 老家 | Lao Jia

OLYLAC

Cockle Pickers: Cao Chaokun

Who will see us
In this foaming sea
Who will hear us
In this howling wind
Who will pull us
From this tide faster than a horse
Who will close our eyes
That won't shut
Until my soul reaches the other shore
Highroad of the bitter sea
Please send my bones home
Under the knotted dragon-eye tree

Cockle Pickers from Morecambe Bay

February 5, 2004, on the eve of the Lantern Festival, twenty-three Chinese workers, age eighteen to forty, drowned while picking cockles at Morecambe Bay beach, England.

Two years later, I stand on that beach. Isaac Julien, the British filmmaker, has invited me here. He's making a movie on immigration. He wants a poem for his project.

Morecambe Bay stretches miles into the Irish Sea. The mud, sediment left by the ice age, feels soft under my bare feet. The sea is distant and calm. Who would know that the tide comes ferocious and fast, and no human can outrun it, not even horses or tractors? Local fishermen fear it. So do the immigrants.

But they came anyway. The only job they could get was to pick cockles in the dark and sell them, nine pounds a bag, to restaurants. The beach was cold, and job back-breaking, yet they came. They owed $50,000 to the snakeheads, who held their loved ones back home as ransom. So they came on Lantern's Day, reserved for family reunion and love. Work is forbidden because it brings bad luck. But they came anyway.

The tide came in the dark. The cockle pickers called 999, but the Coastguard couldn't understand their English. They stood on the shore, listening to the screams for help. England watched on TV, as each cockle picker bid goodbye to his or her family in China, as waves rose to their necks, mouths, eyes.

In the morning, the Coastguard found twenty-one bodies in the mud, two bodies still missing, all in one straight line, as if waiting to board a ship to go home. "The most haunting scene," said one guard.

From the mud beach, I look into the bay of the Irish Sea. There's only cold emptiness.

That night, the ghosts visit me in the tiny hotel room in London, twenty-three of them, including the two still missing. They file into my dream, as foam, waves, wails. Trailing after them, the ten drowned immigrants from the *Golden Venture* . . . all came from Changlecun 长乐村, Eternally Happy Village on the shore of the South China Sea, the port where Admiral Zheng He sent off seven expeditions between 1405 and 1433, his fleet containing over twenty-seven thousand crew and hundreds of ships with silk, silver . . .

"Why did you leave home?" I ask. "Changle is a beautiful place on the coast, plenty of fish and farmlands. You work yourselves to death in New York, San Francisco, London, and Amsterdam, send your money home to build mansions that remain empty, because everyone is busy making money abroad. It doesn't make sense."

They weep and disappear into foam. I wake up. In my notebook, there's a drawing of spiraling waves—in each wave, an eye, a mouth, a hand, a name, a soul, drifting towards home.

So the tragedy of the cockle pickers is the tragedy of every immigrant, also mine. Their desire, their death and hope is also mine. Their struggle at Morecambe Bay is my struggle at New York. Their dream to have a better life is also my dream. Our lives are entangled, through ten thousand waves. Our story must be told and heard, through ten thousand waves.

I call Isaac. "I need to visit Changle, home of the drowned victims, home of the Chinese immigrants around the globe, home of the seafarers."

It takes me a year to write the poem. Each stanza is named after the drowned from Morecambe Bay . . . Each word is uttered to raise the dead from the ocean floor, down the mountains, across the deserts . . . to guide the souls home.

Isaac calls from London. He's raising new funds to make a nine-screen film installation. He wants to name it "Ten Thousand Waves," a line from the poem "Cockle Pickers." And the poem will run through the film as its story line, its spirit, its spine.

Cockle Pickers: Xie Xiaowen, Yang Tianlong

On the night of the Lantern Festival
We stream into the sea
Jumbos, craams
Three-forked prongs
The wind bites our ears, hands, and toes
Home, we say, home
And tears streak our rubber sleeves
On the night of riddles and light
The moon is full behind thick clouds
We cockle, cockling
In the quicksand of Morecambe Bay

dust angels

stars, diamonds, tears of hearts
sand and cut, cut and sand
shrouded in silicon fog
we string beauty with cornhusking hands

bracelets, necklaces, rings
day and night, night and day
we bend over screeching wheels
making trinkets for the U.S.A.

saints, gods, Buddha
rush down the belt at a dizzying speed
a quarter-cent apiece—price
of our hands, a nation's pride,
a civilization eating us alive

opal, malachite, topaz
stones from deep in earth—sold cheap at Walmart
our lungs harden from quartz crystals
our lives weigh less than dust
we cough and wheeze
walking half a block we gasp for air

they say we fake our sickness
have never worked in their factories
they hire lawyers to erase our names
ban our union. no more Marx or Mao
only golden path of market economy

no money to go home
no face to see parents or children
all bridges collapsed—
we loiter in hospitals, courts
we pray not to die in this strange land

dust angels, dust angels
who wears the stars and hearts strung with our tears?
who makes a fortune from our wretched breath?
who will see us—
of all the Buddhas and saints
carved out of our bodies
all the eyes of Mary and Jesus
painted in our blood

Cockle Pickers: Xu Yuhua, Liu Qinying

Tossed on the communist road
We chose capitalism through great perils
All we want is a life like others
TVs, cars, a house bigger than our neighbor's
Our boy in a better boarding school
Now the tide is rising to our necks
Ice forming in our throats
No moon shining on our path
No light for our orphaned child
No exit from the wrath of Morecambe Bay

Hakka Man Farms Rare Earth Metal

First of all, it's not rare nor earth, as they call it.
The metal lies under our feet, sparkling in the soil we farm,
Red, green, yellow, blue, purple, land of grass
And buffalos, patches of rice, bamboos, sweet yams.
We came here as guests—Hakka—fleeing from angry
Lords. Year after year, we bent over the earth
Feet and hands in the neon soil, our sweat
Fertilized the fields, children, ancestors' graves
Our stove cooked the fragrance from the sun and moon.

Now we dig, deep in the mud, our boots
Rotting in the rainbow sludge . . . Dig
And we dig, hoes, pickaxes, guns, explosives
Acid wash, ten yuan a sack, this red dirt
Speckled with blue and yellow.
Home, we cry, a small haven painted with green.
Now the mountains are lifted.
Deep crates in the fields, blood and pus
In streams and rivers . . . all because the world
Wants this earth—"Vitamins" for iPods
Plasma TVs, wind turbines, guided missiles—
Things that make the world
Cleaner and more beautiful, as they say

And here we are, in the waist-deep sludge
A sack of mud—a tale of greed
Leaching in our stove.
Fire licks my wife's slender hands
Acid fumes in her lungs, liver, stomach
Till she can no longer sip porridge laced
With the thousand-year-old egg.
In our cooking woks, we exhume
Dysprosium, Neodymium, Promethium
All the names of Gods, they say.

If Gods have eyes, would they see us
Slaves on this earth?

In the distance, a mushroom of dust—
Boss and his Prius, powered by the sludge
That chokes my eyes, ears, nose . . . One *Rich Field*
twenty-five pounds of metal, ten thousand sacks of earth
Ripped from under our feet. We're slipping,
Our chests soaked in blood, backs broken
Digging, pulling, no food or water.
Our quota still short, the boss will be mad,
But no matter. I light a cigarette, each puff
Is the last. Tomorrow is gone, like our village.
Here and far away, where horses once ran wild
Under the sky, where we, children of
Genghis Khan, return every night in our dream
which is gone, too, they say. Mongolia,
Our origin, now a rare earth pit for the world.

Oh, Hakka, Hakka, forever a guest
Wandering on this bare earth.

Cockle Pickers: Lin Zhifang, Yu Hui, Wen Ge

We know the tolls: twenty-three—Rockaway, NY
fifty-eight—Dover, England, eighteen—Shenzhen
twenty-five—South Korea, and many more
We know the methods: walk, swim, fly, metal container
back of a lorry, ship's hold
We know how they died: starved, raped, dehydrated
drowned, suffocated, homesick, heartsick, worked
to death, working to death
We know we may end up in the same boat

Boy at Sea

I met Boy as his interpreter. My colleague Jim was representing him for his asylum application. Boy didn't speak English. Jim needed him to practice his answers before the judge. So he asked my help for the mock trial.

Boy arrived with tea as gifts for us, tins of Tieguanyin 铁观音, Iron Bodhisattva, the best Wulong tea 乌龙茶 from his home province, Fujian. He looked like a skeleton. Jim said he was still recovering from his thirty-day hunger strike in an Amsterdam prison in order to get out and come to America for asylum. By law, the Dutch government had to release him after he lost sixty pounds. They sent him to prison because they didn't believe he was a refugee, didn't believe he was fifteen. His lawyer and interpreter, appointed by the government, told the judge that all Asians look like teen refugees. The judge sent him to prison for lying and illegal entrance as an adult.

Before Amsterdam, he'd been jailed in Italy, France, Germany . . . for the same reasons.

Before he reached Europe, he had spent a year drifting in the sea.

Before that, he was home with his parents. On his fourteenth birthday, the parents fled arrest for attending the underground Catholic Church. A month later, his uncle took him to a sailboat, told him to run because the cops were coming for him. His parents had borrowed \$50,000 to pay snakeheads to get him to New York City, via South Asia, Europe, then America. Once he arrived, he'd work in restaurants to pay off the debt.

His uncle didn't tell him the journey might last for years, with jails, hunger strikes, beatings, rapes . . . There were stories. But stories were luxuries they couldn't afford.

At sixteen, Boy still looked fourteen. The traumas didn't age him. During our practice, his face turned in the direction of the South China Sea, the direction of home, Changlecun 长乐村, Village of Eternal Happiness.

I asked Boy what he'd like to do when he got his asylum. He smiled, for the first time.

"I'll call mama and papa, and tell them I'm a free man now. I can go to church whenever and wherever I want, and I'll go back to school for my diploma."

And he told me how he crossed the line.

How To Cross the Line

*Any alien who is **physically present** in the United States . . .*
may apply for asylum—INS § 208

First you gather the paper:
Plane tickets, photos, letters, passports
All fake but for yuan, euros, pounds
Fake certificate, fake license, fake face
Everything about you, even the names
Round them up with care
Tear them, shred them, chew them
Flush the pulp down the toilet
Before the plane touches the ground
You come out clean as blank paper
Belong to no country, no race, man or woman
You're on your own
Bleached, in the mirror
Listless, no hair grown
On your phantom face that is not
Yours—the fear, the hunger, the thirst
The urge to throw yourself
On the ground and cry *Mama*

No!
You walk along the thin corridor
Along with the fellow passengers in suits and perfume
Who rush toward customs, baggage claims
To the shadows hovering behind opaque glass
Bouquets, homecoming banners, limousines

And you stand in line
You choose a booth with a woman officer
Pudgy, pasty white—a contrast to the young
Starved body that's not yours
You look around
The girl from Fuzhou, still a skeleton
From the two-week hunger strike in Amsterdam
Has picked an obese man

Her tender ankles curve like talons
Over there, under the neon flickering CITIZENS ONLY
You see the man behind the line—
Poised to jump
Dyed beard, dyed hair
The scar on his temple pulsing red
A lighthouse leading you across
the Indian, the Atlantic, the North Sea
His lion fists kept you safe from snakeheads
In the holds of rusty ships
You want to throw yourself at his feet
Uncle Wu, where have you been?
I'm WX, Remember me?
But you freeze, your face a mask
Like his, hers, and others
Whose names you must erase
From your sixteen-year-old soul

Suddenly I'm alone
Before me, no human shield
Behind me, no exit for escape
To jump or die—STOP
Breathe, slow, deep
Pat pockets one more time
Everything set—no baggage, no name
No memory—only this body
No longer mine, never mine
Having crossed endless borders and seas
For this final sprint

The officer looks up
Eyes shadowed with overnight fatigue
A smile on her face and your knees buckle
In that small second—Mother
Will she be on the other side—the land of plenty?
But her finger is up: NEXT
And you push—a puppet
Pulled by an invisible string

The smile recedes from her eyes
Ripples of shock, fear, alarm
Push
Carrying nothing—everything
Past her booth, her yellow line of authority
Past the guard huffing over, gun in hand
Pushing
—a fetus—
Crying ASYLUM

Cockle Pickers: Wen Ge, Chen Aiqin

父母在, 不远游
父母在, 不远游
父母在, 不远游

When father and mother are around
Children do not wander far from home

Lao Jia | 老家 | Old Home

At sixteen, my father ran away from his widowed mother, to fight the Japanese.

"I'll come back with a Ph.D. and serve my country with better English and knowledge," I pledged at the farewell party in Beijing, 1986.

Home—家—*Jia*: a roof under which animals live.

When asked where I'm from,
I say "Weihai," even though
nobody knows where it is,
even though I've never been to the place.

He lost his left ear in a bayonet fight with a Japanese soldier. Two years later, American cannons split his eardrums.

The bag lady stopped her cart on the busy street and peed onto a subway grate.

"Did you jump or fly?" asked my landlady from her mah-jongg table. Then she laughed and told me that her husband had jumped ship ten years ago. When he opened his fifth Chinese take-out, he bought her a passport and flew her to Queens.

The only thing he liked to talk about was his old home, Weihai 威海, its plump sea cucumbers and sweet apples, men with broad shoulders, thick thighs, and girls with long braids making steamed bread.

"Back home, I had no money, but I never felt poor," she said, shivering behind her fruit stand. "Here, if my money goes down below four thousand dollars, I panic." She scanned the snow-covered streets of Chinatown. "I guess I really don't want to be homeless here."

I hired the babysitter when she mentioned her hometown was Weihai 威海.

The president visited the rice paddies in Vietnam, where a pilot had been downed thirty-three years ago, to bring his bones home.

My father tried to return to 威海 after his discharge from the Navy. With his rank, he could find work only in a coal mine town nearby. My mother refused to go. He went alone, and got sick with TB. Mother ordered me to date the county administrator's son so he could help Father come home.

"No, I'm not sad." The street kid shook her head.

"How can I miss something I've never had?"

On her sixtieth birthday, my grandma went home to die, sailing from the island to Shanghai, from Shanghai to Yantai, then two buses to Weihai 威海. I carried her onto the big ship at the Shanghai Port, down to the bottom, where she'd spend three days on a mattress, on the floor, with hundreds of fellow passengers. "How are you going to make it, Grandma?" I asked. She pulled out a pair of embroidered shoes from her parcel and placed them between my feet. "My heart and liver, come to 老家 soon, before it's too late."

House—*房—Fang*: a door over a square, a place, a direction.

He never lost his accent, never learned Mandarin or the island dialect.

威海, a small city
in Shandong Province,
on the coast of the North China Sea,
a home, where my grandfather
and his father were born,
where my grandma married,
raised her children, and
now lies in the yam fields,
nameless, next to her husband,
an old frontier to fend off Japanese pirates,
a place I come from, have never set foot on.

It's my 老家, lao jia, old home.

Back from America, my mother furnished her apartment on the island, bought a new one in a suburb of Shanghai, and is seeking a third in Beijing. “A cunning rabbit needs three holes,” she wrote to us, demanding our contributions.

They swore, before boarding the ship, that they’d send money home to bring more relatives over; in return, they were promised that if they died, their bodies would be sent back home for burial.

I drink American milk—a few drops in tea.
I eat American rice—Japanese brand.
Chinese comes to me only in dreams—in black-and-white pictures.

My mother buried her husband on the island of the East China Sea, where he lived for almost fifty years, after he ran away at sixteen, from his old home on the Yellow Sea.

Room—屋—*Wu*: a body unnamed and homeless until it finds a destination.

We greet a stranger with
“Where are you from?”
When we meet a friend on the street, we say,
“Where have you been? Where are you going?”

家—a roof under which animals live
房—a door over a square, a place, a direction
屋—a body unnamed and homeless until it finds a destination

—tangled roots 根 for wandering souls.

Cockle Pickers: Wu Hongkang

We pat the sand, we pat the sand
Teasing cockles to the cold surface
We dig, we pick, we break our backs
Bagging cockles for two pounds
They say we can return
When the bag is full
But home is far away
In the dark, we can't make out the sea
No stars point our path to the shore
Wind comes from all directions
Cutting our bones
How empty is desire
In the foaming mouth of Morecambe Bay

II. An Immigrant Carol

An Immigrant Carol

I arrived at JFK on the night when the Mets won the World Series. My host drove me through Flushing, trying to explain what it meant to win a World Series, but my head spun with only one question: How am I going to make it in New York with twenty-six dollars in my pocket? Yes, I knew English, from Beowulf to Shakespeare to Poe, but I couldn't make out a single word from the streets, couldn't understand why people went crazy over a ball. Then I heard my sponsor say:

"Ping, tomorrow you'll start working at my antique store, so you can go to classes at Long Island University at night. Five bucks an hour, so you'll have money to rent your own place. Prove yourself worthy, yes? Not easy to get you out of China!"

I tried, but I was clueless about American culture: UPS, subway, baseball, football, rock-n-roll, jazz. Eating pizza and hamburger, I threw up. I wouldn't wear make up, or put on the old dresses and lipstick my sponsor's wife tossed on my bed in the basement. Soon she declared I was lazy, stupid, ungrateful, and must leave, now!

Three days after arriving in New York, I was on my own.

I wandered from borough to borough, Queens, Bronx, Brooklyn, looking for a cheap room and an under-the-table job to pay for food and rent. Only Chinese restaurants would hire me as a waitress, because they don't pay wages, so no tax or immigration troubles. I worked for tips, and I got fired constantly for being too slow, too plain looking, for making mistakes adding up the bill, or simply being too "uppity" because I was in grad school. In less than three months, I had six jobs in all boroughs, and moved four times, Brooklyn, Harlem, and Queens. I lost twenty pounds, my face was inflamed with hives. I cried myself to sleep every night, asking why I'd given up my teaching job at Beijing University to live a dog's life in New York City.

On my first Christmas Eve in America, I was kicked out again from a Chinese restaurant on Fifth Avenue. The manager seated a German family of six at my table. They seemed polite, took a long time studying the menu, ordered eight items, and ate them all. After they rushed out for a Broadway matinee, the manager called me over, threw the bill in my face:

"Stupid cow, how dumb could you be! Your Peking University degree went to your ass or what!"

A $104 meal, and the German didn't sign his credit card.

I dug out the tips I had earned that week plus what I had in my wallet. I was still eleven dollars short, but the manager grabbed the money and pushed me out into the howling wind. The streets were empty except for last-minute shoppers. They were all rushing home for Christmas, gifts under their arms. My home was a tiny unheated room in Flushing, emptier and colder than the streets. And I no longer had the rent money to pay the landlady, who was waiting for me in the kitchen.

Despair froze my eyes, hands, feet.

I walked past MoMA and opened its glass door, hoping to warm up before they threw me out. *Lily Pond* welcomed me. It was Monet's *Reflection of Clouds* series. I'd written an essay on this painting for my art class at Beijing University, but this was my first time to be with the original work, and my knees went limp. I sat down on the bench and was transported to the lily pond in Paris. The tight knots in my neck, shoulders and hips began to unwind. The ice in my eyes started melting. I could breathe without feeling the choke in my throat.

I sat with Monet till a hand touched my shoulder. "The museum is closed, miss." I looked up. It was a guard, tall, thin, olive skin, and dark hair.

"First time here?" he asked, kindness in his brown eyes.

I nodded.

"First Christmas in New York?"

I nodded again. Tears started pooling in my eyes.

He took my hand. “Please come and have Christmas dinner with me and my friends on Staten Island. My name is Rob. I’m from Greece. My roommates are from Iran, Italy and South Africa.”

I stood up and followed him. On the ferry, I asked: “Why so kind? You don’t even know my name.”

He smiled. “I know you. It’s written all over your face, also on mine. Tonight, we wear the same nametag for the holiday banquet: Immigrant.”

The sunset touched the Green Lady’s hand. She raised her torch and lit up the entire bay. It set my heart on fire.

For the first time since I arrived in New York, I felt hope.

I smiled, my first in America.

The Story of the *Golden Venture*

In 1993, I met Ai Weiwei 艾未未 in the East Village, at a meeting to help the victims from the *Golden Venture*. The cargo ship traveled four months from China to Africa to New York City, carrying 286 Chinese in its hold, then ran aground in the sandbar of Rockaway, Queens. Ten of them drowned in the sea, six of whom are buried in a New Jersey public cemetery, because no one came forward to claim the bodies. The rest, hundreds of them, were languishing in detention centers.

I told Weiwei I was thinking of traveling in a smuggling ship to experience the journey firsthand so that I could write the story, and I'd need to raise $40,000 to pay for the trip, but if I had that kind of money, I could use it to help the victims and their families . . . so I was torn. Weiwei smiled as he listened to my rambling, then introduced me to the work of Tehching Hsieh, whose year-long performance art "Cage" required mind-blowing endurance, determination, and passion. He also introduced me to his roommate Xu Bing, another Chinese artist known for his "Book from the Sky."

Art is a honey badger. You don't give up until the job is done, at any cost, he said.

I couldn't raise $40,000 for the trip.

Meanwhile, I was invited to perform with Allen Ginsberg at the Poetry Project. I decided to write a poem for the six drowned immigrants buried in New Jersey, because no one would take them back to China for proper burials. Because they were not properly buried, their souls had become wandering ghosts in a foreign land, forever seeking ways to go home. I wanted to visit their graves, but I didn't drive, so I begged my friend to take me there in his car. We kept getting lost even though John was a Marine, a trained navigator. When we finally got close, a storm came out of nowhere. The sky turned pitch dark and we had to pull over until it cleared.

By the time we got there, the cemetery was closed. Through the fence, I promised the souls that I'd do my best telling their story.

I wrote, no food or sleep for five days. I went on a voyage with the dead. They shared their longing, sorrow, humor . . . "The Ghost Song from the *Golden Venture*" was complete. I lost vision for twenty-four hours. I knew I had given my best.

I read the poem next to Allen, who performed "Howl." Clayton Eshleman published it in *Sulfur*. Adrienne Rich selected it for *The Best American Poetry* . . .

I thought my words had given rest to the dead souls.

But what did I know?

And what did I know of what was still to come . . .

Calling Ghosts from the *Golden Venture*

so here we are
in the evening darkness
of Rose Hill Cemetery
gazing out from our ghost eyes
like the homeless outside windows
no moon
the spring not the spring of the old days
our bodies not ours
rotting in the grave of lao fan 老藩
we look at the sky
the earth
and the four directions
the storm gathers in
from all sides
how shall we pass this night?
the wind comes blowing
we six
in deep shadow
stand at the end of time
stand in the night
that is not just an absence of light
but a persistent voice
unsteady and formless
hum of summer crickets
something wants to be said
even if our words
grasp the air in vain and nothing remains
our story sets a fact beyond fable
our story has no beginning or end
"home," we say
before we utter the word
our voices choke with longing
the cliff of Fuzhou
studded with stiff pines
the waters of Changle
shadowed in the swaying bamboo

sea and sky fused
mystic fires along the shore
fishermen's dwellings everywhere
how lovely
how familiar
when dusk falls
faint seagull cries
blue smoke rises
from red-tiled roof
small boats offshore
and fish hawks in silhouette
salty winds
carrying murmurs of reeds
tide roads of the sea
the scenes grow in memory
scenes we lived day by day
paying no mind
generation after generation
nets cast into the lingering light
seeds planted in morning mist
fishing kept us out on the waves
farming bound us to the earth
but at times
we heard a voice, a promise
a golden dream
things seen and heard
turned to confusion
we pulled our boats onto the shore
left our wives and children
behind mountains' shadow
from village to village
we bought and sold—anything at hand
socks underwear suits shoes gold drugs spirits
seven days a week
three hundred sixty-five days a year
and not just for money
the yearning for adventure
ran deep in our veins

we played hide-and-seek
with government and police
when we got caught and lost our proceeds
we called ourselves "Norman Bethune"
if Mao were still alive
he might even praise us
for helping build up China
as he praised that Canadian doctor
who gave his life fighting Japanese ghosts with us
still, waves of desire
rose daily
this voice luring
from far side of the sea
not that we desire gold
or world delights
but this voice
first muttering
then roaring in our heads
so in hope and fear we fared
in tears we fared
mist spread a veil till ocean-bound
pinewood mirrored in deep green
in the hold of the *Golden Venture*
we did not see our women weeping
did not hear our children calling
only the voice
kari, kari . . . of wild geese
we sailed the ocean
in the hold of the *Golden Venture*
pigs chicken dogs snakes
whatever it was they called us
our bodies not ours
sold to the "snakeheads" for the sea
you ask why we did this?
ask the geese why they migrate
from north to south
why the eels swim thousands of miles
to spawn in the sea

tides of desire
rise for no reason
so we fared with faith
New York had more *fu* than Fuzhou
people there enjoyed “perpetual happiness”
like the name of Changle 长乐
so we sailed with the belief
we could buy ourselves back for $30,000
within three years
our hands would bring freedom
to our sons and grandsons
prosperous and happy
not like us, cursed
by our own country, cursed
by lao fan 老藩—old barbarians
America needed our labor and skills
as much as we needed its dream . . .
and here we are
hovering around this New Jersey cemetery
our bodies gone
but our souls still hanging
like curtains soaked in rain
our summer clothes so thin!
so thin our dream!
hovering . . . that dark night near Rockaway
our ship heaving into sight of New York
in thirst and hunger we waited
in fear and hope we waited
to be lifted from the ship’s hold
alight on the land of paradise
“jump,” we’d been told
“once your feet touch American soil, you’ll be free.”
in the dark rain we waited
“jump,” someone shouted
“the ship is sinking, the police coming!”
so we jumped
into the night
into the raging sea

our breasts smothered
by foam and weeds
our dreams tangled
with despair and hate
breath beaten from bodies
oh, we've sunk so low!
how low we sink!
only to rise again
clinging to illusions
easy to sink
in the fire of desire
regret comes after the deed
sorrow!
our days now changed
leaving no trace
the distant mountain lies alone
shadows of the city so far away
sorrow!
we can speak only in weeping
memory nothing but white hair on the heart
condemned to wander
lost among the roots of our six senses
gazing at New York
gazing homeward
who can avoid sorrow in this world?
our legs lingering
in the dew-drenched grass
here and there, still clinging
this deep night
is it outside this world?
our women and children
still awaiting our return
but here we are
nameless
in life and after life
apart
our song is the crane
calling in her cage

when she thinks of her young
towards nightfall
will it reach Fuzhou and Changle
and stir souls from their sleep?
on the boat
we were close
hundreds of us in the hold
jammed in and in
here we live even closer
six bodies in one hole
the earth sifting into
our common grave
unmarked
no stone erected
then crumbling
sands of the shore
may reach and end
but not our grief
home, oh go home
an empty wave
ten thousand voices
broadcast the pain
please, oh please call our names
Chen Xinhan, Zhen Shimin
even if you can't say them right
Lin Guoshui, Chen Dajie
even if you don't know our origin or age
Wang Xin, Huang Changpin
please, oh please call us
raise our shadows from the moss
be gentle as you call our names
do not wake us by force
but call us
do not let us fade
from this place
unlit
unfulfilled

Cockle Pickers: Chen Aiqin

Every night since I left home
I've been folding a boat
To rest my aching bones
How thin is the paper
Paler than winter
A boat full of bleeding hearts
Home—all the heart wants
Is to be called home again
From the silent Morecambe Bay

The Last Call from Aleppo

It's Christmas Eve and snow covers Aleppo
As it covers the rest of the world
Please remember my child under the snow
Under the metal and concrete of Aleppo
No one comes for us: No UN, no Red Cross
Only tanks, planes, cluster bombs
As the bell tolls for Christmas
The world watches us in silence
Our homes shattered bomb by bomb
Our schools crushed plane by plane
Our hospitals demolished tank by tank
Our children buried alive in powdery concrete
Their cry choked before it reaches the sky
As superpowers bicker over who owns the world
Oh, what happened to us, to be born
In such a wrong time and wrong place?
What humanity could allow this cruelty?
What sanity could allow this blood bath?
What civilization could witness this annihilation?
Please hear my daughter, her last plea for a hand
If my child is your child
If my mother is your mother
If my sister is your sister
If my home is your home
If my city is your city
Could you sit still in the silent night of Christmas
And watch us perish under the rubble of Aleppo
Into the crashing waves of the Mediterranean Sea
As the bell tolls from the ruins of Aleppo
From the snow-covered ruins of humanity?

Our Prayers on Father's Day

Dear God, we are not child actors. We are children. Real children.

Dear God, where is my papa and mama? We just walked three thousand miles, fighting coyotes along the way. We thought we'd be safe once we crossed the Rio Grande.

Dear God, you said everyone is born equal, every life is a gift, and the kingdom of heaven resides in the mustard seed.

Dear God, we are small and young. Some of us just learned to walk, some still wear diapers, and some are still nursing. Are we not your tiny mustard seeds, dear God?

You say a kid must not be boiled or eaten in mother's milk. Why are you ripping us from our mother's breasts, from our father's hands?

Dear God, we have lost everything: Our country, our home, our friends and tomorrow. We have nothing left but our papa and mama. Please give them back.

Dear God, here's my mama's number. Here's my papa's number. Here's my aunt's number. I have them memorized. Please call so we can get out of this dog kennel.

Dear God, you cried for donkeys moaning under loads and falling on the roadside. Are you crying for us, as we fall off *La Bestia*, crushed under *El Tren de la Muerte*?

Dear God, you wept when you heard starving baby ravens crying from the nest. Are you weeping for us, Lord, as you hear our wailing for papa and mama from the cage?

Dear God, we followed your law to flee from danger: A burning forest, a roaring tsunami, a raging war, violent gangs.

But, dear God, it's been months since I was yanked from mama's breasts, since I'm left in the cage, crawling in circles . . . as I turn the tender age of eleven months old.

Dear God, we didn't want to leave home, walk three thousand miles, or fall off *La Bestia*.

Dear God, we are not criminals or child actors. We just want our mama and papa. Our parents are not criminals or actors. They just want to raise us. There's no script. Our only word is to live, like all God's children.

Do not turn the light off on us, dear God. Do not throw away the key to our cage. Give back our papa and mama, dear Lord. Do not forsake us, alone, terrified, drowning in our tears. Hear our cries on Father's Day. Hear the cries of our fathers and mothers, dying from the death sentence of separation.

Dear God, please let us be children again, like arrows in the hands of a warrior. For we're your mustard seeds, your heritage, keys to thy kingdom of heaven, dearest God.

Note: Ann Coulter claims that twenty-three hundred children in cages are "child actors," and the Democrats gave them scripts to read and cry about their suffering.

Cockle Pickers: Wang Minglin

Ten thousand waves
Push me to the shore
My son skips rocks on the rolling sea
Will he hit me, a bodiless soul
Foam among endless waves
Will he raise a lantern on my path
A soul bodiless
Floating in the seething Morecambe Bay

Broken Intestines: A Honduras Story

I stumbled upon his name. In the media storm of the family separations, his death was just another ripple. But his spirit took over my hands, heart, liver, intestines . . . till I became his vessel to get his story across the abyss. I didn't research him till I finished. Everything I wrote or auto-wrote about this man and his family matched what I found later. Mr. Muñoz was a Honduran refugee from the Copán River, where the Mayans built their civilization. He had lived in America before, worked, married, raised their first son, then moved back to the Copán River to grow coffee, until the gangs threatened their lives and they had to flee to the southern border, where he was separated from his child and wife, where he died in jail.

I was shaken to the core, but not surprised. The souls possessed my body and auto-wrote their stories through my hand, heart and spirit: in "A Ghost Song of the *Golden Venture*," "The Cockle Pickers," "Who Killed Soek-Fang" and others.

Still, who am I to cry on Mr. Muñoz's behalf, on anyone's behalf?

Who gives me the voice and hand?

Who struck Rilke with thunder so he could write *Duino Elegies*, after ten years' silence?

What hand took Kafka into a cockroach's world and wrote his way out?

What drumbeats led Gary Snyder to Zen, the Turtle Island?

What do we do when the door to the other world swings open, and a voice commands: *Enter, listen, and bring our story back to the human world?*

Writing is telling.

Telling is hard. Telling in a second language is harder. Telling in another voice, from another world, in the right manner and heart, takes huge tolls on the body and mind.

I'm in perpetual pain from the telling.

My ex said I carry the weight of the world on my back, and it was crushing him.

But I don't have a choice. The voice chooses me, as a conduit, to feel, cry, breathe, write, so I can live, so we can live.

Call me appropriator, call me possessed, call me fraud . . . as long as my heart is in the right place, my voice anchored to the earth, the story will rise to the stars where all elements are connected, all sounds mingled, all lives matter.

Poets are shamans, moving matter from spirit to spirit, ghost to ghost, transporting dreams from boat to boat, poem to poem, star to star.

Duan Chang—断肠—Broken Intestines

—Voice of Muñoz, Honduran asylum seeker in Texas border jail

I know home—*nah*, a hut under banana leaves, in the *tocar* rising five hundred feet above rainforests, on the bank of the Copán River, in the valley of Mayan ruins.

I know Ch'orti', my Rosetta Stone to unlock Mayan history, my father, mother going back two thousand years, through *tzutz*—feathers of macaws—for the sky, through *chan ti*—snake mouth—for the underworld, through my blood—*ch\ich*, through my bones—*b\ ac*, through my ashes—*tan*, to reach my wife and children—*sitz*.

I know water—*ha*; I know lake—*eha*; I know rain—*haha\r*;
I know river—*xucur* that runs with tears and blood for my *sitz* yanked from my chest.

I know teeth—*eh, cha\m*; I know tongue—*a\c*; I know mouth—*ti*. When ICE tore my son and wife from my bleeding fingers, when my *eh*, *cha\m*, *a\c* are ripped one by one from my *ti*, I become *cha* and *tun*, stones grinding stones in *xucur* of *pococ*—river of dust.

I know liver—*xemem*; I know heart—*alma*. When *xemem* and *alma* are torn out of me, what's left to keep this body alive?

I know a heart can repair itself, but not intestines broken by sorrow.

This is a tale from China, three thousand years old.

> A fleet sailed along the Three Gorges to fight a war. One soldier caught a baby monkey and kept it on board for his amusement. Mother monkey followed the ship along the shore, no food, no sleep, only howls. The soldier found that amusing, too. On the tenth day, when the army docked their ship, mother jumped on board, held the baby in her long arms and dropped dead. Soldiers opened up her belly, and found all the intestines broken, every inch of it, bleeding sorrow. When the commander heard the story, he had the words branded on the soldier's forehead:
>
> ***Man Guilty of Robbing a Child from a Mother***

Monkey had followed her captured baby for days with no food or sleep. It was her birthright to be with her child.

Birds and fish migrate thousands of miles across borders. It is their birthright to seek food and pass on genes.

We flee from death and hunger. It is our birthright to feed the young and old.

We love our rainforests, our *tocar*, *ha*, *eha*, *xucur*, *haha\r*, our macaws, bats, frogs, orchids, bananas, coffee, our slums on hills, our ruins and pyramids. We've tried your land of soy, corn, McDonald's, meat packing plants, slaughterhouses. Our first son was born in America. We got homesick and returned to the Copán River, to our coffee beans and banana trees, until gangsters killed my wife's brother and came after us.

So we walked, two thousand miles, through Guatemala, across Mexico, to seek asylum.

We rode *The Beast*, the *Train of Death*, fighting robbers, fighting hunger and shame.

We followed the North Star. We marched towards Mother of Mercy.

After Guatemala, we lost everything we carried from home. After Mexico, we lost our shame. All we want is a shelter, food for our *sitz*, and the reunion with our first-born in America as we cross the Rio Grande, into Texas, with nothing but our bones and hope . . .

Who'd know the Land of Free has become the land of kidnapping? Who'd know that our birthright to hold our children would be stripped once we cross the border? Who'd know you'd quote the Bible to exonerate your cruelty?

I know bark—*pat*; I know skin—*pat*. I know children's *pat* is their mother and father. They die if you strip their skin.

I know the Book of Exodus:

> *Do not boil a kid in his mother's milk.*
> *Do not eat a kid cooked in his mother's milk.*
> *Do not benefit from a kid soaked in his mother's milk.*

I know burn—*pur*; I know breast—*uchu*. When I watch a four-month-old ripped from *uchu*, mouth still dripping with milk, when ICE pries my baby from my hands, when my *sitz* weeps for me in a cage, my *pat pur*, my *alma mb\ar*, my *xemem* bleeds, my intestines break, my whole being a slow burn from *oc* to *hor*.

I know rope—*succhih*; I know neck—*nuc*. I twist my shirt into *succhih* and tie it around my *nuc*. I roll and roll until my breath is no more. I let go my flesh to awaken my jaguar spirit. It leaps from my temples and bursts through the cage to catch up with my *sitz* and their mother. My spirit lifts five hundred feet high, to shine moonlight on their path.

Who'll brand the tattoo on the forehead of America:

> ***Man Guilty of Kidnapping Kids in the Name of God***

The jaguar is speaking, his words splashed with my *ch\ich*, from the pyramid summit.

My *uc\ab\a* is Marco. I'm Honduran. My *wixca\r uc\ab\a* is Orlanda. She's Honduran. My *sitz* are Hondurans. We see with same eyes, smell with same noses, speak and eat with same mouths, feel same joy and sorrow with our *alma*, our sweat pours into *rum* for the same reason you plough the earth. We love our kids the same way you hold your *sitz*. Our hands reach for the same hope like yours. Our *sitz* are not pets you can steal or lock in a cage. We're children of Mayan spirits and jaguar warriors, of *q\uin* and *e\c* and *rum*, our pyramids built to petition gods. Let us live. It is our birthright to live, like the sun, moon, earth, and all the stars.

Common words in Ch’orti’ language

all: tuno\r
bark: pat
bite: ac\uhxop
black: negru u\t
blow: uyuhta
breast: uchu\
child: sitz
cold: insis
cut: xur
die: cham
dog: tz\i\
dry: taquin
ear: chiquin
eat: we\
eye: naq\uiu\t
far: naht
fear: ap\a\cta
fingernail: or uyoc
fish: chay
fly: top
foot: oc
full: b\ut\ur
good: imb\utzop
hair: tzutz
head: hor
heart: alma
here: tara
horn: cachu
husband: noxip
kill: chamse
know: na\t
laugh: tze\n
left: utz\ehc\ap
liver: xemem
ashes: tan
big: nohta
bird: mut
blood: ch\ich\
bone: b\ac
burn: pur
cloud: tocar
come: yo\p
day: ahq\uin
dig: impahni
drink: ch\i
dust: pococ
earth: rum
egg: cu\m
fall: c\ax
fat: ch\ichmar
feather: tzutz
fire: c\ahc
five: inmohy
fog: mayuhy
four: chan
give: ahc\
green: yaxax
hand: c\ap\
hear: oyp\ica
heavy: mb\ar
hit: tz\ohy
how?: tuc\a
I: en
knee: pix
lake: eha\
leaf: uyopor
lie: ch\a
long: innaht
meat: we\r
mountain: wítzir
name: uc\ab\a
neck: nuc
night: acb\are
one: in
person: winicop
rain: haha\r
right: wach\ c\ab\
road: b\i\r
rope: ch\a\n
rotten: oq\uem
sand: hi\
seed: hinah
sing: c\aywi
skin: pat
smell: chuchu\ co\c
stab: inxeq\ue
star: e\c
stone: tun
sun: q\uin
swim: nuhx
that: yaja\
thick: pim
this: ira
tongue: a\c
tooth: eh
two: cha\
warm: inq\uin
wash: pohch\
we: on
what: tuc\a
where?: tia\
who: chi
moon: uh
mouth: ti\
near: nut’ur
new: tapop
nose: ni\
other: inmohr
pull: nquerehb\a
red: chacchacop
river: xucur
root: wi\r
rope: succhih
round: gororoh
say: a\r
see: wira
sit: turu
sleep: way
smoke: b\utz
stand: wa\r
stone: cha\
suck: catz\upi
swell: asampa
tail: neh
there: yaha\
thin: jay
thou: et
tooth: cha\m
tree: te\
walk: axanop
wash: poc
water: ha\
wet: cuxur
when?: tuc\a dia
white: sacsac
wife: wixca\r

Note: Vocabulary above taken from the Wikipedia page on Ch’orti’ language.

Cockle Pickers: Guo Nianzhu, Yu Hui

Our hands ache from cramming
Our feet are numb in winter's clutch
Indeed, we long for home—yuanxiao dumplings
On the night of the New Year's full moon
Steaming hearts of sesame, red beans
The sticky skin seals our bad deeds
In the tongues of gods
Oh, home—pining of the soul
The moon has completed many a cycle
But not our dream, listless
On the foaming Morecambe Bay

Boy in America

It's been ten years since Boy arrived and requested asylum. He got the best lawyer, pro bono. He got many judges, some sympathetic, some suspicious, some grumpy. He practiced hard for each court appearance. He was granted asylum by a retiring Minnesota judge. Two days later, a new judge squashed his jubilance, who took over the case and revoked the asylum grant. His reason: The police letter summoning the Boy was fake. The typewriter that produced the letter had produced similar letters for many other asylum seekers, therefore, the judge declared the letter moot. Boy appealed, failed, appealed again, failed again, appealed again, all the way to the Supreme Court.

I watch his face age with each trial, from baby hairless to mustache fuzzy to beard sporadic . . . His back stoops more each time I see him. He sleeps, eats and works 24/7 in restaurants in New York City, New Jersey, Florida, wherever there's work, however he can save money to pay back that $50,000 loan for the snakeheads. His feet drag more with each trip to see his lawyer in Minnesota. He's been wearing ankle bracelets for ten years.

When his last appeal failed, he said,

"If you don't hear from me, it means I've gone under, gone dark—*hei* 黑."

He caught my eyes glance at his ankle bracelet and laughed. "It's not hard to get rid of them."

One morning at three thirty, I got a collect call from a Florida detention center.

"Please tell Jim I'll be deported back to China within twenty-four hours. I wouldn't have minded leaving. I'm tired of hiding, but I have a two-year-old boy now, and another one on her way. How's my wife going to take care of the kids and restaurant alone?"

So Boy has paid off his debt, married, become a father and restaurant owner.

He's now living his hard-earned American Dream, without his "paper," in ankle bracelets.

All shall be smashed within twenty-four hours.

I called Jim. In his half-sleep state, he miraculously found the new policy from the Obama administration. It allowed children who entered America under a certain age to stay in America. Boy's age and year of his entrance fit that category. He became one of the 800,000 DACA dreamers.

Boy was released and allowed to stay with his family, to run his restaurant.

He never got his diploma, never had the chance to go home, to let his aging parents meet his wife and children.

He prays every Sunday morning with his family, in a local church, in his ankle bracelets.

China Wok

Chop chop chop
A chicken under the cleaver
Headless, no feathers adorning its breast
The new President has spoken
No leniency no America no asylum
Go home, Boy, go home

The sea is blue outside the window
The hurricane rains into my eyes
Swollen like home on the other shore
Where's home? Where's Mother?
Father? Six years on the run. No voice
Where's my bitter tear? Only spider webs
Seal the stove, the Bible, Jesus on the door . . .

Swish swish swish
On the cutting board, flaking scales
Mouth wide open, eyes that won't close
If the fish could speak, what story would it tell?
If the 800,000 dreamers had a voice
What cries would we utter? The bell rings
And rings from the tower. Children
Laugh as they circle on the grass
Presidents come and go, but not our dream
Oh Father, Oh Mother
Which basement are you in, kneeling under the cross?
What psalm throbs from your chapped throats?

In the headless breast, the heart beats
Into swelling waves, drifting like bait
I don't know how to swim or fish
But I keep throwing the thin line of hope
Whoosh whoosh whoosh
Oh, Mazu, Goddess of Mercy
Please hear my story, a boy homeless
Since fourteen, a boy floating from sea to sea
In the holds of rusty ships, a boy on hunger strike

In an Amsterdam jail, then London, then Pisa . . .
A boy crossing the border to seek asylum, a boy
Working seven days a week to pay off
$50,000 to the snakehead. Ten years
The boy is becoming a man
Still homeless, still an orphan, still dreaming

Whoosh whoosh whoosh
The chicken is frying in the wok
Who sees me boiling in the wanton oil?
Who hears the whimpering sea of anguish?
Who will judge me, a boy with the same
Buffalo heart and Mayflower dream
That made this land, this sea, this America?

Cockle Pickers: Lin Guohua

The lichee tree we planted is blossoming
White flowers hide under dark green
The first moon comes and goes
But I haven’t returned as promised
Lanterns, riddles, yuanxiao dumpling
Lion dance, songs, children on stilts
My love hovers in the deep shadow
Lotus lamp on the tree, unlit
Who will wipe tears from her lichee face?
Who will sail me home from Morecambe Bay?

Buried on Christmas Eve

During Tuesday night's State of the Union address, Representatives Alexandria Ocasio-Cortez of New York, Ilhan Omar of Minnesota, and Rashida Tlaib of Michigan wore pins bearing the image of seven-year-old Jakelin Ameí Rosmery Caal Maquin.

Jakelin Caal Maquin was seven years old from Guatemala. She developed fever soon after she was separated from her father at the border. Within thirty-six hours, she died of cardiac arrest, brain swelling and liver failure.

Seventeen days later, Felipe Alonzo-Gomez, an eight-year-old boy from Guatemala, died of cardiac arrest, brain swelling and liver failure within thirty-six hours, soon after he crossed the border.

Both children were indigenous Mayans; both left their impoverished mountain villages; both walked two thousand miles with their fathers to seek a better life; both were healthy when they arrived at the border, both separated from their fathers by ICE; both suffered from fever and vomiting after the separation, both died sudden deaths within thirty-six hours, after being diagnosed with a "common cold."

Felipe breathed his last breath minutes before Christmas in a U.S. border clinic, as the villagers buried Jakelin in the high mountains of Guatemala.

How frequently can a common cold kill? How fast can a common cold kill?

I ask these questions from my years of medical training, my eyes flooding with tears, my conscience torn apart, my heart bleeding, my hands picking up the pen, my throat singing "Silent Night" till the words fill the sea . . .

Silent Night

—For Jakelin, Felipe and all the children at the border

Silent night, holy night
All is calm, all is bright
In a border hospital, a boy, nameless
No father or mother to hold his hand
No media knows or cares about his name
He's just another boy from Guatemala
Who walked thousands of miles, to stay alive
A boy so tender and mild, so innocent
As he exhales his last breath into the hands of ICE
Twelve minutes to midnight, before the Day of gifts and joy
A boy laid bare, alone, terrified
On this holy night, on this silent night

> Sleep in heavenly peace, boy eight years old
> Sleep in heavenly peace, boy from the Q'eqchi'
> Sleep in heavenly peace, boy who died in the land of promise

Silent night, holy night
All is calm, all is bright
In the village of San Antonio Secortez
A girl is laid to rest in wet soil
Her father still locked in Texas jail
Her mother too ill to lower her coffin into the earth
The bell rings and rings
The Savior was born, the Savior is asleep
She's another girl, seven years old
Who walked two thousand miles with a dream
Only to be crushed at the border
As she is laid bare, without mother or father
In the mud, alone on a cold, cold mountain
A girl so tender and lively, so innocent
On this holy night, on this silent night

Sleep in heavenly peace, girl seven years old
Sleep in heavenly peace, girl from the Q'eqchi'
Sleep in heavenly peace, girl who perished in the land of plenty

Wark, Felipe Alonzo-Gomez,
I found your name buried in the news
Wark, Jakelin Caal Maquin,
I won't let you vanish in the fog of lies
Wark in heavenly peace,
good Maya k'ajols from Guatemala

All is not calm or bright
Until we raise your names from the grave
Until we awaken the Savior from this grave of hypocrisy

Notes on Mayan Q'eqchi' vocabulary:

1. *K'ajol: children*
2. *Wark: sleep*

Cockle Pickers: Wang Xiuyu

I have no time
To make love to my wife

I have no time
To watch my son grow

I have no time
To feed my mother

What Marwan Carries across the Desert

He carries a bag, tattered memory of his mama and sister
He carries dust, thousands of miles from home in Syria
He carries tears, plaster dry on his cheeks, wrinkled from desert sun
He carries pleas, scratched from his sand-filled throat

He's Marwan, four years old

Born to play marbles, run around all day
    with his siblings, playmates
Born to get dirty, get into trouble and get yelled at
    by his loving parents
It's not his job to play hide-and-seek with soldiers,
    armed to the teeth
It's not his job to teeter through the desert,
    too tired to lift his eyes
Too understanding to call his papa
    to wait and hold his hand

He carries hunger, thirst, loneliness

He carries the question why he is walking in this
    godforsaken desert
He carries the fear that his family will soon vanish from his
    downcast eyes
He carries the weight of the century that abandons him,
    his parents, his country

He's Marwan, four years old
Born to beg mama for one more good night song
Born to beg papa for one more lift into the sky
It's not his job to carry the tragedy and war in tattered plastic
It's not his job to carry the sorrow and failure of humanity

He carries the chasm of twenty steps separating him from papa
He carries the greed of superpowers and corporations and politics
He carries the nonsensical violence of this epoch
He carries the conscience and despair of civilization

He’s Marwan, four years old
Born to raise his eyes to the stars,
    asking ten thousand questions
Born to wonder and marvel at the world,
    its unfolding magic of love

It’s not his job to limp through a desert in despair
Not his job to slant his tiny body to support the weight of violence

We’ve failed you, Marwan, four years old
As your mother, father, brother, sister . . .
As a poet, professor, human rights expert, empathy maker . . .
As a country, as a species, as democracy and all the lofty slogans

But I swear, Marwan, four years old
To all the sand under your feet
To every tear drop on your face
I shall not let you wither in the desert
We shall not let you perish in the void

The Names You Call Me

You call me "Criminal,"
as you cheat, assault, and rob the world blind.
You call me "Shit-hole,"
as you foul the Earth with your lies, runoff, toxic smoke.
You call me "Welfare,"
as I work day and night, no vacation, no complaints.
You call me "Thief,"
as you dodge tax dollars in billions.
You call me "Rapist,"
as you grab my Mija by her genitals.
You call me "Animal,"
when ants and bees know more discipline than you.
You call me "Murderer,"
as you snatch my children, freeze them to death in cages.
You call me "Violence,"
as you shock and awe with drones, Mother of All Bombs.
You call me "Lazy,"
as I build your roads, railways, factories on my knees.
You call me "Not Good Enough,"
as my awards pile higher than your white rage.
You call me "Slum,"
cooking, gardening, cleaning in your bloody mansions.
You call me "Marx,"
igniting hope and equality among the wretched.
You call me "Worst,"
as students nominate me year after year for awards.
You call me "Whore,"
breasts laden with milk, buttocks curving like the Amazon.
You call me "Terror,"
my arms taller than the Andes, thighs smashing your shackles.
You call me "Mao,"
freeing China from your opium wars and colonial lootings.
You call me "Dog,"
"No Chinese Allowed" in Shanghai's Concession Parks.

You call me "Che,"
    whistling Amazon warriors from my jungle breasts.
You call me "Monster,"
    pulling the poor, the sick and the homeless out of the muck.
You hunt me with ICE,
    troops, Coast Guard, Proud Boys and white supremacists.
You call me "Uppity,"
    spending millions in court to put a Chink in the Chink place.
You send students to destroy,
    enraged for praising black, brown, yellow poets.
You shun me as the "Pariah,"
    ban me from campus for life.
You build the Wall,
    blocking my path to cross, work, speak, write, publish, live.
You call me "cavalier, liar, paranoid, renegade, crazy bitch,
    detached from reality . . ."
You call me "Mandela,"
    Twenty-seven years in jail, still singing with dignity.

You cut my veins, opening lava of rumbling spirit.
You shackle my feet, and I gnaw through the hole with teeth.
You slit my throat, and I summon songs with dance.
You kill my birds, and I build a temple with feathers and stardust.

You can kill my birds, slit my throat, shackle my feet, bury me alive, cut my veins, block my path, hunt me down with your drones, lawyers and lies . . . my body is not my body . . . my name is not my name . . . I belong to every Mija and Mijo, to the Himalayas, Andes, Rockies, to the Nile, Amazon, Yangtze, Mississippi, to the four seas . . . call me your Monster, Terror, Animal . . . call me Mao, Marxist, Che, Mandela . . . names blown, blowing with the wind . . . but nothing can change this: I'm your Amazon, your Everest, your Pacific . . . I'm your Sky and Earth . . . I'm your parents on the road . . . your children in cages . . . named or nameless . . . I'm Truth that defies your lies . . . I'm Conscience that jolts you awake in a cold sweat . . . I'm Poetry that sails hope across the sea and desert.

Cockle Pickers: Zhou Xunchao, Dong Xiwu

we
move
with the
sea: currents
of plankton, eels, turtles
the sea carries us to the land
of gold. We're urchins under
prickly needles. With a tender
heart we ride currents, following
Polaris—our destiny always
the same: to feed the old
and young, to rest by
the
yellow
sea
in
peace

III. immigrant can’t write poetry

immigrant can't write poetry

"oh no, not with your syntax!"
—a harvard professor to a chinese poet writing in english

she walk to mountain
she walks to a mountain

she walk to mountain now
she is walking to a mountain now

what difference it make
what difference does it make

in nature, no completeness
no sentence really complete thought

language, our birthright and curse
pay no mind to immigrant syntax

poetry, born as beast
move best when free, undressed

Cockle Pickers: Guo Changmao, Zhang Xiuhua

Tread the sand with care
In the tangled weeds
There are hungry ghosts
Tread the waves with care
In each foamy mouth
There is a word
Tread the words with care
In each howling sound
A soul, unfulfilled

父
母
在
父母在　不远游
不
远
游

Of Mice and Mankind 人鼠之间

"It was a turning point for me, when my professor grabbed the lab mouse and flung it against the wall."
—Biology Professor

And you have tears in your eyes
As you depict the hand to our class
Pale, hairy, unapologetic
The hand of a master
And the lab mouse, blind, cancer-ridden
Yet happy to be a mouse, still alive

Then the rage, out of nowhere, the fling
Against the wall, and the spine, the brain
The heart, splashing like asteroids

It awakened something in me, you say
Tears in your eyes, *I'm no longer the same*

As you watch the human "mouse"
In the teeth of the revenge machine
Invisible, raged, raging
The same spine, muscle, limbs, bones, brain
—Genes that share 99 percent of your DNA
Flung across your path

As you stand in the ruins
As you walk through this razor sharp silence
As you wade into the bloody sea of sacrifice

Are you willing to say: *It awakens something?*

And say: This hand, this yellow, brown, black hand
Makes the same delicious meals
Makes the same beautiful sonnets
Splits cells with the same precision?

Are you willing to acknowledge
Our milk is just as white and nourishing
Our blood just as red running through same veins
And our need to be human or mice is just as legit?

How do you keep the same
As you watch this human mouse
Who breaks bread and knowledge with you through the semester
Who's now flung against your wall of conscience
Over and over and over . . .

Cockle Pickers: Guo Binglong

The water is up to my chest
The boss got the time wrong
I can't get back in time
This is my last call from the sea
Oh darling, can you hear me
Through raging waves
Washing me to the bay?
Can you see me from the yam fields
As you gaze towards the sea?
Who will unclench your fists
That feed our son, our aging parents?
Ten thousand apologies
My wind-chapped beauty
Pray for your ill-starred man
Wailing from the forbidden Morecambe Bay

She Shall Not Be Moved

—A Golden Shovel after Gwendolyn Brooks "To the Diaspora"

you order me to grow up and stop throwing "rage" around. **your**
secretary scorns and scolds and sets up roadblocks for my **work**
then reports them as proof of my yellow chaos so **that**
your excellency can summon me to explain why I **was**
a *challenge* for everyone. who's everyone and what have I **done**
apart from making "stars" with my blood? what evidence **to**
back the charges you can't name? *moxuyou*—shadow daggers—to **be**
lodged in my organs. I was your poster babe, my art has **done**
you much glory, now I'm a ghost—unseen, unheard, unspoken **to**
just because I said *no*. if this is your justice, let it **be**
flooded with truth. if this is your grown-up world, then I'm **done**
with your game of bigotry. let me sing in agony. to live is **to**
fulfill a child's dream. let her play, shake the earth and sky. let her **be**
your mother of conscience. she shall not be moved till the job is **done**

Notes:

1. *Golden Shovel is a poetic form created by Terrance Hayes in homage to Gwendolyn Brooks' poetry. A line from her work, "To the Diaspora", is used here in bold words: "Your work, that was done, to be done to be done to be done."*
2. *Moxuyou: A Chinese term from the Song Dynasty (twelfth century), describing how the Emperor charged his general Yue Fei for treason and killed him based on lies. The term has become synonymous for baseless rumors, charges, allegations, etc.*

The Peacemaker

—For Kieu Linh, who died for ninety minutes from hemorrhaging after a miscarriage while fighting for her tenure, then returned to tell truth.

I know pain—whips in air, slicing the flesh
I know scars—keloids mapping the skin
I know hunger—scavenging food for the old and young
I know cold—breaking ice with frost bitten hands
I know work—24/7 till passing out from exhaustion
I know silence—steely eyes from wall to wall
I know rumor—vermin rolling from tongue to tongue
I know slander—snake in tall grass
I know sneer—daggers into liver and spleen
I know fear—worm holes in the brain
I know loneliness—free spirits since birth
I know torture—top down, bottom up, inside out
I know shock and awe—its mushroom cloud
I know death—journey to hell and back
I know mercy—in the sea of violence and greed
I know light—in the tunnel of despair
I know love—fuel from the earth core

I know phoenix . . . rising from the radioactive dust

Cockle Pickers: Lin Guogang, Lin Youxing

Ten thousand waves
Call our mother
Sorrow
A statue facing the sea
Raven hair bleached by salty wind
Go home, Mother
The shore is empty, the net
Tangled under your feet
Go home
Pray for your sons
Buried in the grave of Morecambe Bay

Who Killed Soek-Fang 素芳?

A Singapore-Chinese scholar, taught International Studies at a liberal arts college. She didn't pass her third-year review and died of breast cancer shortly after she was dismissed. She was thirty-five. When the lawsuit broke, my lawyer cried, had a nervous breakdown, then washed her hands of me. No other lawyer in town would open their door to me. Soek-Fang came to my dreams, three nights in a row. I started digging, and unearthed the truth: She was an award-winning scholar, a beloved teacher and mentor. I wept and wept. I had never questioned the lies used to fire her: She was a dumb teacher and scholar . . . till the same lies are now being used to kill me.

I

I'm breaking through this Tower, 素芳

We have toiled
With our bleeding dream
On our knees, from our deathbeds
No holiday, no weekend, no vacation
No time for friends or children
Only our vita bigger than this nation
Only this yearn to be seen
As something "good enough"—barely

I refuse to believe this powdered lie—
"Not good enough, will never be good enough"
Because of our accent, our immigrant hands and feet
In this fruited plain

I refuse to let doubt seep between your eyebrows
Into your breasts, heart, liver, spleen, throat
Till every drop of blood, every cell of our being
Is filled with this cancerous thought:
Are we good enough? Will we ever be good enough?
Under the purple mountain majesties
I refuse to fill our vita with bone marrow
Honors, awards, books, and students
Testifying how we've changed their lives
Under the beautiful halcyon skies

I refuse to swallow this poison
That has been killing you, me, us
Across amber waves of grain

II

June is your month, 素芳, and you showered us
With gifts from gods: flowers, sunshine, laughter
A bird of paradise, a tropical bliss to Minnesota-nice
One couldn't find a mean bone in your supple beauty
In June, we traveled from St. Paul to Taiwan, Nanjing, Shanghai
International Seminar on a mission of equality and justice
Your heart already shrouded by toxic rumors
My eyes already fogged by doubt and smirk
Yet you stood tall, in your Golden Cock Stance
Under the Peace Gate of Nanjing
Where 300,000 souls, raped then slaughtered, moan day and night
You kept your head high
Even when cancer had tunneled into your breasts, our minds

Thank you, 素芳
For coming to me in my darkest nights
With your lion heart and silver sword
To forgive my ignorance and awaken me with light
To keep my dream alive in this land of free
To fuse your warrior spirit into my limbs
To tear down the façade of hollow slogans
To urge me telling, in verse and deeds
What's happening to us . . .

Thank you, 素芳
Your sword is humming for bloodstained truth
One story, one ripple, one wave
Two stories, two ripples, two waves
Till they form a tsunami—
A tsunami of love

To bring down the alabaster tower
To free our sisters, our children
To dance again under the June sun
In the land of free and beautiful

III

I'm rising, 素芳
We're rising, Soek-Fang
If the law won't speak justice
We sing it with our poetry
If justice becomes a mask for lies
We burn it with our eyes
If their lies smear our spirit
We cleanse it with our blood
If our spirit can't cross the chasm of hope
We make wings of seven billion hearts
To fly from sea to shining sea

Fear is no longer an option
Silence is no longer an option
Take our hands, 素芳, rise with us
From sea to shining sea
Under the beautiful halcyon skies
Over the purple mountain majesties
Across the amber waves of grain
Through this fruited prairie
Till we reach the land of the free

IV

In the golden palace of Wells Fargo, a settlement is signed and sealed as "mutual understanding," a check to gag the truth that keeps rising and rising.

Beneath the mantle, magma rumbles: what gives light must endure . . .

I’ve lit the match to a parched prairie
I’ve scorched a path through the jungle
I’ve burnt the dome of *The Hunger Games*

I’ve spoken—
Yellow Plague from China, toppling the Tower and still standing

V

It’s mid-April. After a tormented winter
The last blizzard falls on the Old Man River

Kate comes over and we walk into the wet snow
Carrying the weight of the entire Mississippi

Trees bend into lizards, crocodiles, wolves
An eagle leads us to robins, owls, yellow finches

We chat about kids, schools, divorce, race
We follow the footprints of turkeys, foxes, coyotes

At the confluence, Fort Snelling is besieged with spirits
Cries of Dakota warriors peal from Pike Island

Far away in Ramallah, poet Ghassan Zaqtan
Vows patience, his fever for love and beauty

So breathless, the earth trembles under our boots
The river whirls, its dervish skirt swelling

We pause. A silence has taken our breath
And I know you’re here, 素芳, keeping us alive

Cockle Pickers

Who will see us
In this foaming sea
Who will hear us
In this howling wind
Who will pull us
From this tide faster than a horse
Who will close our eyes
That won't shut
Until our souls reach the other shore
From a raging Rockaway
From a distant Morecambe Bay
From sealed cargo holds, lorries, trucks, vans . . .
Oh, highroads of the bitter sea
Please send our bones home
Under the knotted dragon-eye tree

Blind Sight, Hidden Brain

Few police officers ever face trial for shooting deaths [of blacks] . . .
let alone are convicted.—CNN

No one said the N-word or Chink
But those pale eyes that dissolve us
Into thin air, eyes that cut sharper than steel
Pulverizing our reason to live

To see is to believe. In order to see, there must be light. Light enters the eye. Nerves transmit the world to the brain in fragments, upside down. The brain flips them back with a reconstructed story.

On the stage, their only job is to hand the right envelope to the right hand, a job easy enough to do with eyes closed, and that's exactly how it was done. With a sleight of hand, the moon is switched, the thunder stolen. And the world can't believe its eyes.

So many lies
In the sleight of hand
In the eye of the beholder

The eye sees what it wants to see
The hand has its own vision

Bacteria is a camera eye, turning with the sun like a sunflower. Our eye is a single-lensed camera, with pigments for red, blue, green.

Eyes sparked the Cambrian explosion. Whoever sees can live. Whoever sees more controls the sea. This is how trilobites got their compound eyes, shaped like towers, helmets, balls, shaded, spiked, lidded, horned, as eyes developed in the Cambrian sea, as life exploded on earth.

Vasili Arkhipov, the Russian officer in the submarine, cast a blind vote that saved the world from a nuclear holocaust.

He died quietly, kidney failure from radiation exposure.

The Nobel Peace Prize went to Kissinger, for dropping more bombs on Vietnam than all the bombs in WWII combined.

Dragonfly has thirty thousand lenses
Capturing thirty thousand images in each eye
Its 360-degree vision bigger than the brain

The Eye of Horus maps the mid-brain
Eyebrows—corpus callosum
Iris—thalamus
Stem under the eye—hypothalamus
The wave line—medulla oblongata

We think we have empathy. We claim we love colors. Yet our eyes see a gun when a black hand reaches for a teddy bear; we sweat only for a white hand pricked by a needle.

Tamir Rice carried a toy BB gun to the park
Within two seconds, cops shot the twelve-year-old boy

Sea urchin spikes are packed with photoreceptors
Its whole body is one spiky eye

Humans have eyes for three colors only. Mantis shrimp see sixteen.

This is how a film works—
The eye fills in gaps between moving images.

This is how bigotry works—
The mind fills in gaps with fear and hatred.

After the stroke, he lost his conscious vision: No more visual imagery, no more image in dreams, yet he walks through obstacles without tripping.

The Russian submarine hides in the deep Caribbean Sea, all connections severed. The Americans drop depth charges left and right of the hull. They don't know this sub has a tactical nuclear torpedo bigger than the bomb dropped on Hiroshima. The sub shakes with each explosion. The captain believes the nuclear war has begun, and he doesn't want to sink without a fight. Finger on the button, he demands that Vasili, the second in command, approve the launch.

The evil eye, placed in the center of a palm
Becomes Hamsa, Hamesh, Guanyin . . . the All-Seeing Eye

The visual cortex is cut. The brain no longer sees, but the body still knows. The face smiles and frowns, the hand knows how to trick and what to grab, the feet know where to go, all guided by blind sight, in the sea of unconscious eyes.

Are you seeing what I'm seeing?

Cockle Pickers: Wu Jiazhen

Lichees blush on the young tree
Birds and bees feast with children
My love lingers under the clustered fruit
Her skin sags from too much weeping
Tides ebb and flow with the moon
Our house is empty, covered in tall weeds
I walk on the sand, eyes on the sea
Who can fill the hollow hearts
In the bottomless Morecambe Bay

Ten Thousand Waves

1. Cockle Pickers at MoMA

"Ten Thousand Waves" comes to MoMA to celebrate the twelfth anniversary of the dead from Morecambe Bay. The film has traveled to major museums around the world, and the filmmaker made fame out of the drowned. At MoMA, only those with leisure and money can watch the film featuring famous people like Maggie Cheung 张曼玉. The drowned souls can't join the party. The immigrants from Chinatown work 24/7, saving every penny to pay off their debt. They can't bear watching their dead consumed on the nine-screen spectacle.

As the spectacle woos and wows the audience, as the filmmaker floats on Cloud Nine in full glory, twenty-three souls still linger on the floor of the Irish Sea, waiting to go home, like the ten souls from the *Golden Venture*, six crammed in unmarked graves, longing to 回家. They have no idea the cargo ship that brought them to New York now lies under the Caribbean Sea as an artificial reef for divers, and that business is good.

I linger outside MoMA, on streets, across seas and deserts. I pray to give the souls an eye, a hand, a direction, a flicker of light for their journey home.

But my song alone is not enough. We, immigrants and children of immigrants, must tell and retell their story, our story, until we can return.

回家
Hui Jia
in each word, a mouth
in each mouth, a word
in each word, a hand
in each hand, an eye
in each eye, a wave
to bring home all
wandering
ghosts

2. Ghost Chant

Today the first moon is full again for the year of the rooster
Today we've been dead for over a decade
picking cockles at Morecambe Bay
Lanterns are lit, riddles posted, sweet dumplings
wrapped for wandering souls

For twelve years, you've been churning our story into art
For twelve years, you've been powdering your face with our dust
For twelve years, you've been building your empire upon our bones
For twelve years, you've been pawning our story to museums and media
For twelve years, you've been selling our body for
grants, awards, investments

Upon our hands your art is made
Upon our eyes your fame is established
Upon our feet you travel the world in luxury
Upon our tombs you claim victory for your monopoly

Today our body is not for sale
Today our body is not for catharsis
Today our body is not to be cut, framed, sold

From the bottom of the sea
We rise

Look at us
Look at us
Look at us

Hear us in the cry of your children
Feel us in the flesh of your ecstasy
Taste us in each morsel of your delicacy
See our shadows, flickering
In the deep of your conscience

Pity the Nation

—After Ferlinghetti

Pity the nation whose freedom melts faster than Arctic ice
Whose justice defends sex predators and puts children in jail.
Pity the nation that sells academia into corporate fiefdoms
Whose presidents scream "Not enough"
with their billion-dollar package
Who hike up tuitions to shackle students with debts
Who turn professors into adjuncts and intellectual slaves.
Pity the nation branding youths with Divide & Conquer logos
Who get rewards for ordering WOC professors to
"take down the syllabi!"
Calling them "racists and appropriators" as public shaming.
Pity the nation whose education becomes "just business"
Its giant machine squeezing hefty tuitions
from Chinese and other Asians
Who sell blood and kidneys to send their children
to America for a degree.
Oh, pity the nation whose president churns lies like popcorn
Whose students get presidential awards for libeling
Elders from the Rez
For yelling "you should feel lucky I find your words
good enough to plagiarize"
To her professors who try to teach academic integrity
Pity the nation as her Lady weeps for children
caged along the Southern Border
Her torch stolen to slow-burn the soles,
palms and tongues of defiant students
Pity the nation that rewards cheaters and mediocrity
That condemns poetry for "manipulating emotions"
That bullies truth into silence
That gags science, deletes data, exiles facts into deserts
That wires classrooms with eyes and ears to break spirits.
Oh, pity the nation that builds its high tower upon the bones of the
Natives, slaves, coolies, Asian American scholars, LGTBQ artists,
immigrant poets . . .

Oh, pity!
Oh, let's pity the nation with actions!
Let's stand together for truth.
Freedom is never free.
It wants our flesh and spirit.
But it's worth it.
Our reason to live

IV. My Name Is Immigrant 我叫移民

ACG

Wandering Souls

Once again
Our blood boils with longing
Children of the Yellow Emperor
King of the Four Seas

Our ancestors wrestled
With dragons, monsters, nine-headed beasts
Their floating cities
Covered four seas and five continents
Our village—yellow kingdom by the sea
Port of grand adventures
If you don't believe me
Go stand on the shore of Changle 长乐
Where the South meets the East China Sea
You'll hear the junks' horns through thick fog
Clashing swords and fine porcelain
Admiral Ho's robe fluttering in the arctic wind
Oh, fire of five thousand years
Ancestral ghosts
Our eyes on the North Star
Our spirits yearning for the sea

Cockle Pickers: Liu Qinying, Xu Yuhua

How tall has our dragon-eye tree grown?
We've promised you, our precious child
To come home when the tree blooms
We'll pick the dragon-eyes and sell them
To pay for your school
But the wind is cold
Our backs are broken from bending over the sea
Cockling, cockling in the quicksand
The sea is rising to our chests
Little boy, please forgive your mama and baba
Forgive the eyes
Decaying in the mud of Morecambe Bay

Pilgrimage

Can't say
    how far it is from Chamdo to Lhasa—
    whether it's 800 or 990 li
Days lost traveling like this—
    three steps, and a long kowtow.
When asked, we smile, faces
    wrinkled like mountain folds
Our eyes sweeping over distant snowcaps
    rivers, paths, zigzagging barley fields
Never trained to count miles or days
    but our body knows
        how to measure rocks, lumps of soil

        Three steps, hands raised before chest, nose, and forehead
        Plunge forward, arms and legs straight
        Raise hands slowly to the sky
        Face buried in earth

This is how we fulfill the vow—
    marking dirt roads from Chamdo to Lhasa
    with our limbs and torsos
We set off on November 10, Tibetan calendar October 4
    leaving our mud house, tent, yaks, and sheep to the neighbor
    entire family on the road, old, young, fetuses in wombs

We love each being as we love our mothers
    not just friends, but also enemies
    not just sheep or cows that give us food
    but also wolves, rats, flies
    not just the sun, moon, grass
    battered mountains, cracked fields
    but wind, clouds, snowstorms, hail
    landslides, flashfloods, earthquakes

We set out, fifteen in total
    vows in our breasts, on our shoulders
        where the warrior god lives and the lamp burns

Three steps, full prostration
    A year, a month, three days
The river filled, dried and refilled
    roads packed, deserted, packed again by merchants
Can't say how many mountains we've climbed
    how many rivers crossed, nights spent sleepless
        gloves frozen to our hands
        sheepskin gowns torn to shreds
Can't say how many wooden pads have splintered in our hands
    how many calluses and frostbite on our foreheads
On the road of faith
    words are blasphemous
Only the six sounds
    —Om mani padme hum—
    treasure of the lotus lake
    music of truth

How tired we are—
    three steps, and a long kowtow!
After each river, each peak
    we measure the distance with a rope and made up the prostrations
        No cheating on the ritual
How tired!
    Three hundred thirty-nine days
In the distance, two sick men fall behind
    their gray shadows pressed against the mud road
        A lone wolf lurks, awaiting its final leap

We are tired—
    skin hangs around our bones
    eyes recede into sockets
We stand, between the sun and earth
    hearts throbbing in the fever of faith
We take on the pain of each being
backs bent with this terrible weight
Yet we stand—
No cry of complaint or hate
no gesture to show off such a glory

We stand
to go down again to touch earth

Wind blows against our cheeks,
whispering doubts into our ears:
What if there is no tomorrow or afterlife?

But we plunge on
    Our mouths
        kiss the grass, flowers, dirt, footprints
    Our skin
        turns from pale to brown, from brown to purple

On October 15, Tibetan New Year
    we arrive, fifteen pilgrims from Chamdo
        outside the gate of Jokhang Temple
As our hands glide across the stone slabs
    crowds become silent, a path opens in the middle
At the sound of our chanting
    the red temple gate opens
        monks lead us through the yard, into the hall
Under the lotus seat
    we stand still
        redeemed of weakness, of terror
Mountains tower behind, and our singing
    bursts from our throats
        reaching the unspeakable

We stand, fifteen in a row!
Two men gone
Two babies born on the road
Our chanting conjures up a forest
in beholders' chests.
Zhashi delei! Zhashi delei—
blessings from the humble souls
who have shed everything
for a better life

the art of bargaining

this is a pair of handmade shoes
awkward and lovely like the maiden behind the stand
gold peonies bloom unabashed on red corduroy tops
white soles are made of layered cloth
pasted on a door with flour
and let dry slowly in the sun
stitches line dense and neat
like terra-cotta soldiers on battle grounds

this is a pair of shoes
I've been searching for years
the craft my grandma tried to pass on
before I left home for good
without trying them on, I know
they would comfort my calloused soles
heal my fungus toes
let me run like the wind
a sword drawn out of its sheath

and we start to bargain

"ten," she says, "for the sake of destiny
that brought you to this desert town."
"five," I say without thinking,
a trick from my American partner.
"good joke, Big Sister," she laughs,
deep creases trembling on her purple face.
I blush for no reason.
"six then," I say, avoiding her hands
that bring back the memory of Grandma,
her flickering shadow on the wall threading a needle.
"come on, Sister, have some respect."
"ok, seven, can't go up any more.
respect has to be mutual, don't you think?"
"barely enough to pay for the materials, Sis,"
her voice low, wet like the drizzle.
"no mercy," I repeat the mantra drilled into my brain.

"peddlers are good at arousing sympathies.
that's how they make a living."
"eight, then, the highest I can offer.
you peasants are getting greedier day by day."

she raises her hands, ten knotted roots,
ten question marks drawn by children.
"do you know how many nights I stay up
to stitch the soles? Do you see
my fingers? Do you see my eyes? See
my little brother waiting for a bowl
of noodles my shoes could buy?
his hunger does not lie.
my callus does not lie.
we do not lie."

I walk.
I'm not practicing the walk-away tactic
that works like magic.
I'm running from the mirror of her eyes.
"stubborn girl, stubborn girl,"
I murmur to myself,
"it's just a game, just a game."
she chases, thrusts the shoes into my hands.
"you won, Miss. Take them for nine.
what's nine yuan to you, a dollar and twenty cents?
and what's a yuan, less than a dime?
would you even bother to pick it up from the street?"

I put away my victory in a trunk,
never give it a second thought
until I'm pulled out of the line
at Minneapolis customs, maggot fingers
prodding socks, underwear, wrapped gifts,
and there it is—my bargain
red and loud like thunderclaps:
"you saved a dime, Fool,
but lost your soul."

A Beijing Neurologist in Brooklyn

Sit still, you little pumpkin shit-face.
Stop fidgeting. And stop
whining about your sore feet.
If your mother hadn't left you outside
a shoe factory, dumping you like bad luck,
you'd be digging mud and collecting cow dung
in some godforsaken place.
You'd be lucky to have some corn gruel
to fill your stomach, some rags
to cover your ass. And God bless
if your father agreed to send you
to school for two years, just enough
to get a job sewing buttons embroidering
napkins tablecloths at some Chinese-American joint.
You'd be lucky to marry a peasant from another village,
to have a kid within the quota.
If it were a boy, you'd be pampered.
If a girl, you'd be cursed and beaten.
Or if you were pretty, which you're not,
you'd sell your flesh at hotels, bus stations,
become some rich man's mistress.
If you were intelligent, which I doubt,
you might get into a college,
suck up to your professors for a better grade,
always nodding, smiling
even if you didn't understand or agree.

But this is how fate laughs in our faces.
You, a little nothingness, live in a brownstone
in this filthy rich neighborhood, and I,
a venerable doctor and professor,
wait on you from seven in the morning to nine at night
fourteen hours a day, six days a week, for minimum wage.
You pick at your food like a spoiled princess.
Your Gap outfit and Elefanten shoes
cost more than my daily salary—

all because you call some white-skinned
lawyers Papa and Mama, who hardly see you
except on Sundays, who want you
to speak English without an accent and hopefully
pick up a few Chinese words from your nanny.

No way!
Listen carefully, you little hoof.

A whore is always a whore, just
like a dog will never grow ivory from its jaw.
Born in a peasant's sty, you'll always smell
of mud and straw fermented in piss, your eyes
the cutting wind from the Yellow Plateau,
your feet thick, thighs bulging with muscles,
hips wide for labor, sex, birth,
even though at three and a half you still look
like a two-year-old, still wobble
when you stand or walk, the back of your head
flat like the bottom of a pan from the orphanage crib.
Believe me. I'm a doctor. I know.
Once a peasant, forever a peasant,
just as a Chinese remains a Chinese
wherever she goes, even in her grave.

Why are you crying, you little oily mouth?
You're not supposed to understand a word.
Two years in America should have wiped out your past,
erased every memory. But who am I kidding?
A night alone on the cement steps of a factory,
a year spent in an orphanage. They say
the trauma has stunted your growth hormones.
But who hasn't gone through a few things in this life?
I've survived two prisons, three labor camps,
the Cultural Revolution, and now this plight
at age sixty, to become a maid for an outcast
to support my good-for-nothing son and his family.
And I'm still standing tall, defiant.

So Lili, my silly pumpkin face,
wipe your nose and walk.
Time to practice again.
You're stubborn, and proud. Good!
Don't ever let your parents' frown seal your lips.
Don't let their butter and steak mush your brain.
You're Chinese, a Chinese peasant girl.
Now take your steps.
It's alright to stumble, to fall.
Here's my hand.
Take it.

I'm your countrywoman.
I am your MOTHER.

Cockle Pickers: Chen Muyu, Yang Tianlong

Lichees ripen on the tall trees
Its fragrance lasts three short days
My love harvests with rusty shears
A bundle of lichee, a tear-soaked sleeve
They say the fruit cures toothache and heart pain
But who will get me home before she fades away?
They say you get beans if you sow beans
Oh, sweet lichee, is it your fault
I'm still drifting through the bitter Morecambe Bay?

Solstice in Lhasa

What more can you say
Nomad daughter of glaciers?
City has bleached the sun from your face
Eighteen years old with a freckled nose
Hides of yak, barley, sandy wind
Knees stiff from scrubbing toilets
What dreams keep you alive
On the marble floor of Gangkar Hotel?

Drunken tourists and their nightingales
Money is the moon on Lhasa's holy streets
In Beijing a storm drops thirty-six tons
Of dust upon the city of concrete
Nomad daughter from the Black River
What more can you say?
The wetland is becoming a desert
Home for rats, carcass of yaks

The salted tea you brought to my room
Yellow butter afloat from a distant factory
"It's fake but tastes okay.
The real is gone, like snowcaps."

Wind, breath, naked river beds
At dusk, a boy on motorcycle
Comes home with his last herd
Nomad daughter from the Sacred Lake
What dreams keep you going
In the glass cage of illusion?

Before the clouds
Cabs, trucks, mobs of fortune seekers
Behind the clouds
Potala Palace missing its Buddha

Your ancestors are on the road
Nomad daughter from the Blue Treasure Plateau
Wooden gloves and padded knees
Long prostrations into the thin air
Their cry of never-perish ghosts
Calling you to keep the lamp burning, burning

And you shout to me across the street
"Sister, please find me a rich husband in America."

What We Carry to Everest

—To my Nepali porters, my kin

Chairs, tables, doors
Cups, pots, stoves
Rice, eggs, chickens
On the backs, over the heads
Our dokos weigh more than the Himalayas

We are Rais from Kulung
Children of Genghis Khan
Backbone of Nepal
Porting goods through the Nepali Plains

Rocks, metal, cables
Gas, coal, windows
Beds, sinks, toilets
Everything for cafés, restaurants, hotels
Feeding climbers from East, West, and all corners

We are Rais of Mahakulung
Children of the Dudh Kosi
Seven stars from the heaven
We carry her milk from the riverbeds
Up and down, down and up
To quench trekkers' thirst
Along the dusty path to Everest

Tea, beer, coffee
Sugar, milk, chocolate
Cappuccino machine that costs two million Rupees
Luxuries for civilizations
Strapped on our heads
As we inch up, breath by breath
Towards the base camp
Into the Zone of Death

We're Rais from Sagarmatha
Born warriors of peace
Now the "boys" to bring "comforts"
To make riches for our New Zealand lords

Ropes, axes, ladders
Boots, mitts, crampons
Helmets, goggles, oxygen tanks . . .
Wrapped around our necks
Our breaths thinner than paper
Feet and fingers freeze, then rot through sandals, thin gloves
As we tiptoe under the moaning icefalls

We are Rais of Khambu
Knights of Kirati kings
Mountains' backbone
Our feet faster than leopards
Our shoulders stronger than yaks
Our hearts' roar louder than lions
Our spirits higher than sky
As we carry down your waste on our backs
As we dig your roads on our knees
As we lift thousands of you into glory

But who would see our face
Blackened with frostbite as we fix ropes along icy paths?
Who would hear us gasp
Our loads bear down like mountains as we step into clouds
Who would feel our heartaches
As we search valleys for a glimpse of our hungry children
Who would help us get back on our feet
As we slip from trees, rocks, glaciers
Who would pull us
From under the Khumbu avalanche?
Who would say that every path to Everest
Is paved with our sweat, tears, dust . . .

Oh, venerable climbers from all directions
We've offered you the best:
Our dahl baht and lion hearts
Our yak backs and goat limbs
Our spine of Nepali plains—
Straight up and down between clouds and rivers
Our Sagarmatha—"Head in the Great Blue Sky"
Our Chomolungma—"Goddess of Earth"

Please tread on us with care
As you guide your tour clients through our home
Please do not spit in our face
And say "Here you are, Boy"
As you toss coins, old shoes and moldy sweaters
Into our welcoming hands
Please call us by our names
Rais, sons of Sagarmatha
Sherpas, children of Chomolungma
Pride of Nepal, Warriors of Peace
But please, do not call us your "Boys"
Do not leave us in the crevasse of Khumbu ice
As you count your medals
Gilded with our souls

Cockle Pickers: Wang Xiuyu, Zhang Xiuhua

父
母
在
父母在　不远游
不
远
游

Tread sands with care
In each tangled grain
A soul
Tread waves with care
In each foaming mouth
A word
Tread words with care
In each howling sound
A ghost

My Name Is Immigrant 我叫移民

Ai Weiwei is going home. I ask him what he wants to eat for the farewell party.

"Dumplings, plain old dumplings, pork and cabbage," he says.

Many people come, all Chinese, poet laureates, master artists, composers, conductors, professors from Taiwan, Hong Kong, Mainland China . . . It takes forever to introduce ourselves.

When I talk about my new book, Yu cuts in, "I hope writers and filmmakers will stop presenting Chinese and China in such dark, evil images, especially to foreigners. Don't forget, we have five thousand years of civilization. What do they have? Maybe a few hundred years, unless they count the Native Americans? We should never lose our pride."

Song shouts, "But look at us. We are all supposed to be *ren jian*—the cream of this five-thousand-year-old civilization. Yet it is the land with a few hundred years of history that gives us a place to live."

No one speaks. We all have tears in our eyes.

Weiwei sits alone by the window, twirling a dumpling skin on his fingertips. I grab it from his hand, flip it out of the sixteenth floor, sit down and hold his hand.

"Are you all packed?"

He nods.

"Do you have to go back?"

He nods. His father is gravely ill. Growing up, Weiwei had a feisty relationship with his dad, who would smack him with bricks and laundry bats, hoping to beat some obedience into his rebellious spirit. We had quite good laughs together as we exchanged our stories. Now the old man wants his youngest child at his bedside as he lies dying in Beijing.

"Did your father get his old home back?"

Weiwei shakes his head, then nods, then shakes again. His father is China's most famous poet. During the Cultural Revolution, the whole family was exiled to the countryside. They lost everything, including their house, an old style siheyuan. They've been trying to get it back.

Where is he going to live in Beijing?

When are you coming back to New York I want to ask, but remain silent.

Will he return to the city again? He's been living here for years and has a green card granted to him as a Distinguished Artist. The city has been his home. Is it really? I remember his basement in the East Village, the moldy rings on his shower curtain and linoleum tiles, his artwork strewn around, covered with spider webs, his roommate Xu Bing, another renowned artist from China, pale and starved looking . . . Song and Yu are still arguing back and forth if we are better off back home or in exile . . . and why we can't feel home where we live . . . why we forever feel exiled and homeless . . . now my mind goes to Song's studio in Brooklyn . . . his entire place covered with thirty years of dust, droppings from roaches and rats . . . yet in this "grave" home, he makes hundreds of roles of calligraphy, paintings, poems . . . all breathtakingly beautiful, all kept in mint condition.

That's when the revelation hits me: It doesn't matter where we live, what they call us, Pink, Pin, Pig, Chink, Stupid, Ignorant, Low IQ, China Doll, Lazy Bum, Job Thief, Worst of the Worst, Never Good Enough, Go Back Wherever You're From . . . What matters is how we call ourselves, with the joy and pride of coming home 回家 circling home . . . as a migrant, like a bird, a fish, a butterfly, a tree, a weed, an immigrant, as the first man who walked out of Africa and arrived in South China, who became my Chinese ancestors . . . carrying home on their back, in our heart . . .

I am Wang Ping. I am Immigrant, drifting with the Turtle Island, till I become Mino Giizhii Goo Kwe, Good Sky Woman.

Immigrant is my name, our name. And it's a good name.

"What the fuck?!" someone shouts from the street. The dumpling skin has just landed.

We laugh. Ai Weiwei squeezes my hand. There's light in his eyes, and a smile on his lips. It's not his usual mischievous smile when we've done something "wicked," but a knowing smile. The same revelation has reached him too.

"I hate letters, but I'll write to you from Beijing. Let's keep in touch, Ping."

We hug. Our hearts meet then settle, in a magic space where there is no exile, where home resides in the stillness, while everything is in constant motion. We know how lucky we are, still alive after such turmoil. We know each survival is a miracle. We know our miracle is backed by thousands of unfulfilled dreams. The dead are never dead. They live through us. They sing their stories through our mouths and hands. And we have work to do.

I know he wants to keep in touch through living: free, fierce, fearless.

And we've kept our promise.

V. Hui Jia . . . 回家 . . . Circling Home

Mino Giizhii Goo Kwe: Good Sky Woman

"I learned drumming from my father as a baby," says Chief Alvin Mino Ode Baker. "My father learned how to drum from his uncle William Bineshi Baker, the Thunderbird, the Drum Maker, who learned how to drum on the lap of his father as a baby."

He sings an Anishinaabe welcome song. His drum is unadorned, and beaten from much use, but the sound is thunderous and warm, like his singing, like his name, Mino Ode, Good Heart / Thunder Heart.

It penetrates my skin, churning my blood.

Today Chief Al is performing a naming ceremony.

We met in his homestead by Lake Superior. In the womb of the Mother Earth, Al sang through the ceremony. Someone passed me a bag of herb. I sprinkled some on hot stones and sparks rose like fairies, Sindibad named me "Dancing Light." A few days later, Chief Al received a vision and prepared a formal ceremony.

"Bill Bineshi Baker, the Drum Maker for our powwow dance, is my great uncle, but I call him Grand Father, as he passed me his knowledge," says Chief Al. He raises the drum to the light, revealing the intricate patterns of the stretched elk skin. "This powwow drum is our secret weapon for peace. It's the Creator's gift to the Tailfeather Woman, an Ojibwa, while she was hiding under the lily pad from the white soldiers. They already killed four of her sons during a battle and were trying to kill her. The Creator told her she must save herself and her people with the drum and singing. And that's what she did. As she beat the drum, singing and dancing, her people emerged from hiding and joined her. The soldiers stopped killing after they heard their songs."

He lifts the drum and sings again. We join in, moving in sync with his drum beat. Soon, our limbs, voices and hearts move together as one. The ground shakes under our feet.

Is this the secret power of "Ghost Dance" for the Sioux warriors at Wounded Knee? Is it why their drumming has been feared and forbidden for hundreds of years until recently? How can this little drum hold more power over guns, cannons, the unspeakable cruelty and violence unleashed upon this land, and her children in all life forms?

"My ancestors have been living in the Hayward Lakes region of Northwestern Wisconsin for thousands of years," continues Chief Al. "This is our Turtle Island," where we're recognized as Ogichida—'Golden Eagle Warrior'/'Spiritual Warrior,' long before white men came, before it became the Lac Courte Oreilles Chippewa Indian Reservation. We arise from the Star Nation, the Great Thunderbird, like my Great Grand Father, my Grand Father and Father. The Thunderbirds live amongst stars. We're from stars, too, only descend to Earth to teach humans how to live."

Chief Al received his name during a four-day vision quest, and became the eighth Mino Ode in the unbroken chain of Good Hearts.

"And you, Ping, flow along rivers with prayer flags, poetry, beauty and peace. So Mother Earth grants you the name Good Sky Woman, Mino Giizhii Goo Kwe. Mino—Good, Giizhii Goo—Sky Day, Kwe—Woman, Mino Giizhii Goo Kwe."

He takes his necklace off his neck and puts it around mine.

I press the gift between my palms. It feels warm on one side, and cool on the other, like fire and water. I lift it to the light. The cool side is whitish-blue. The warm side shows yellow, orange and red speckles. When my fingers tremble, a flash of green shoots out.

"Opal," I cry. My friend, Jack, a jeweler near Big Bend National Park, took me rock hunting among Texas' ancient volcanoes. He told me it's rare to find opal, rarer to find "precious opal."

"From Mexico, fire and water," says Chief Al. "The light comes from its heart."

I hold the stone to my chest. Its fire pumps air into my lungs, opens my heart to let oxygenated blood into my arteries, into the web of capillaries, where healing happens at the cellular level, where the waste is sent back into my heart via veins. It's a circular river that runs 100,000 miles, wrapping the earth three times. This is my body of river, connected to Chief Al, his wife Lisa, their tribe, their earth and sky . . . through this stone.

"This one comes from Mother Earth. Another gift will come to you," says Chief Al.

He beats his drum again. His song thunders like a big bird flapping its wings . . . Mino Ode: Good Heart, Thunder Heart, Thunderbird.

I bow, my knee to the ground, my palm beating with the pulse of the earth, my head lifting . . . into the wind . . . the sky is breathing.

For thirteen years in New York, I was Penny Wan.

For seventeen years in St. Paul, I was the troublemaker, the pariah of the academy.

Now I am Mino Giizhii Goo Kwe—Good Sky Woman on this good earth.

I offer prayers to mountains and rivers and all life, through thoughts and deeds.

Hui Jia . . . 回家 . . . Circling Home

Every Chinese belongs to *lao jia*, 老家, our native land, ancestor, our food, name, spirit, roots . . .

老 lao: old, origin . . . over the head is *tu*, 土, earth, and a plough cutting through ground to make home.

Every Chinese wants to 回老家, *go back to old home*, or simply, *go home*, no matter how far we wander.

At fourteen, I left home on the big island of the East China Sea. I worked in a fishing village, for the one-in-a-million chance to go to college. I never returned.

Three years later, I left the village to study English in Hangzhou. I never returned to the island.

I left Hangzhou for Beijing University. My college dream came true at twenty-two.

I left China in 1986, to pursue my Ph.D. at NYU. I never returned.

"Go back home!" Americans scream, from streets, colleges, social media. Still, I never went back.

I drift farther away from Weihai, my lao jia, carrying that old earth in my dreams.

Shanghai is my birthplace. Zhoushan Archipelago, 舟山群岛, is where I grew up till seventeen. I studied English in Hangzhou and Beida, 北大. I earned my master's and Ph.D. at NYU. As a foreigner, I taught poetry twenty years as an English Professor at an elite college, the only and last miracle. I've raised my sons, trained poets and writers . . . my old home is still registered as Shandong, Weihai, 山东威海, my 老家, my *earth*, 土; my *heart*, 心; my *liver*, 肝.

For Chinese, the liver stores blood, and the heart moves it, a circuit of paths leading to one destination—home. At night, the blood must go home to restore the soul and settle the spirit. If it can't go home, we have a problem: insomnia.

At fifty, I took my sons to the Yellow Sea. It was our first time to see 老家.

Factories and buildings have taken over the land my father talked about every day. The wheat fields are gone. The village is gone. The sand beach is gone. My grandma's grave still stands in the yam fields. I sit down in front of her stone, and everything floods up: sorrow, joy, bitter, sweet, her stories, handmade bread, noodles and dumplings, my father roaming on the island in search of the immortal reishi mushroom, 灵芝, his longing to go back home, 回家.

I watch my sons eating steamed bread, strung together like beads with a red thread. It is their first time to eat this traditional food, but they devour it as if it has been their daily meal since birth, as if they were slurping Cheerios and milk. This is the bread my father craved while living on the island, while sailing the East China Sea as a commander.

Return—回—*Hui*: a mouth within a mouth.

Is that why there is a Chinese restaurant wherever there are Chinese? Just so we could go back home through our food?

Is that how my sons are tied to their lao jia, 老家, in China, even though they were born in New York City and Minneapolis, love pizza, play hockey and baseball, speak English, Hebrew, and Chinese?

I check the dictionary. 回 = 迴 = return = go home by walking, travelling, wandering on earth, carrying mouths, 回, on the traveller's back, 迴 . . .

I remember my DNA test by National Geographic. 200,000 years ago, my ancestors walked out of Africa, crossing the land and sea, following food, hunting, gathering, making home along their paths, reaching South China after 100,000 years.

I remember my father: Left home at sixteen to fight the Japanese invasion, lived and died on the island in the East China Sea, but in his heart, home is forever Weihai, 威海, by the Yellow Sea.

Just like monarchs, geese, salmon, elephants, weeds and other life on earth, travelling thousands of miles to follow food, but always know how to go back, 回老家.

Home is a transit word . . . 回 . . . 迴 . . . return . . . go home.

I keep digging. I need to find the origin.

What I found makes my hair stand up. In the oldest version of Chinese, when words were carved on the bones of birds and whales, on the backs of turtles, 回 = 回 = water; 迴 = 迴 = water rippling, pushing, whirling, circling towards home.

Home is embedded in the water. Going home is embedded in running water. When Chinese see the word 回 . . . 迴, we've already arrived.

My heart feels at home, finally.

We are water, born to move, wander, migrate, whirl, circle . . .

No need to get mad when people shout “Go Home” at us.

We all carry home in our heart and liver, in our blood, in our DNA, as we flow from continent to continent, from sea to sea, to appease the soul, to circle back home . . .

. . . 回 . . . 迴 . . . 迴 . . . 回 . . . 迴 . . . 迴 . . . 回 . . . 迴 . . . 迴 . . .

Cockle Pickers

父母在　不远游
父母在　不远游
父母在　不远游

游
必
有
方

When Father and Mother are alive
Children do not travel far

But if you must wander
Know where you're going

—acknowledgments—

Many thanks to my women-warrior sisters who trust and support me unconditionally: Caroline Kieu Linh Valverde, Greta Gaard, Reshmi Dutt-Ballerstadt, Carolyn Forché, Jeanne Calvit, Carol Hiniker, Franchesca Flores, Jenne R. Andrews, Izzo Kizzay, Sachiko Nishiuchi, Shannon Russell, Wang Sue, Allison Hedgecoke, Mary Francois Rockcastle, Susanna Vessel Franklin, Ginny Moran, Alison McGhee, Rita Wong, Andrea Jenkins, Ann Finneran, Charlene Chan-Muehlbauer, Katie Tsuji, Rachel Schmitt, Robin Whitfield, Patricia Spears Jones, Louise Taverner, Julie Schumacher, Robin Moede, Pamela Williams, Linda Russo, Elena Favela, Kristin Naca, Pamela Lee, Yang Xin, Ruthann Godollei, Linda Buturian, Sierra Lomuto, Amy Elkins, Jennifer Kwon Dobbs, Soek-Fang Sim, and many others.

Special thanks also goes to: Gary Snyder, Ai Weiwei, John Ruskey, Adam Stoltman, James Lenfestey, Paul Hoover, David Cope, James Sherry, Quincy Troupe, Paul Portuges, Jim Cihlar, Scott Slovic, Ray Wang, Marc Nasdor, David Miller, Jonathan Skinner, Michael Drummond Davidson, Ron Johnson, Sindibad O'Dell, Al Baker, Bruce Bolon, Jonathan Stalling, Paul Mundt, Robert Masterson, Fred Wah, Adhely Rivero, Marcus Green, Joseph Desenclos, David Lawrence Grant, Tommy Lee Woon, Cole Chang, Joe Lerro, Joseph Kessy, Donovan Ernest, Eliot Armah, Patrick and Kevin Conroy, Wagtail, David Schmidt, Scott Gannis, Jesse Katzman, and my sons, Ariel and Leo—my poetry and art comrades, river brothers, mountain guides, and Native relatives—may the rivers and mountains be with you always!

And everyone at Hanging Loose who helped make this book possible—Robert Hershon, Dick Lourie, Mark Pawlak, and Caroline Hagood.

Poems from *My Name Is Immigrant* have appeared in the following books, anthologies, journals, magazines, newspapers, and websites:

The Best American Poetry; *Fight the Tower*; *Big Scream*; *Yellow Medicine Review*; *World Literature Today*; *Black Renaissance Noire*; *Foundry*; *Hanging Loose*; *Poesía*; *Book Riot*; *Chinese Literature Today*; *The American Journal of Poetry*; *Zócalo Public Square*; *Women : Poetry : Migration*; *Poetry*; *The Golden Shovel Anthology*; *DoveTales*; *About Place Journal*; *downstream: reimagining water*; *New American Writing*; *PBS NewsHour*; *Cross Worlds: Transcultural Poetics*; *Berkeley Journal of Gender, Law & Justice*; *Of Flesh & Spirit*; *The Magic Whip*; and *Ten Thousand Waves*.